| The Frilly Girls Coloring Book |

This book belongs to:

_____

_____
Date

© L. Farrell Publishing. All rights. Reserved.

Copyright © 2020 by L. Farrell Publishing

All rights reserved.

ISBN 978-1659078411 (Paperback)

No part of this book may be reproduced, distributed
or transmitted in any means or form including photocopy,
recording or other electronic methods without written
permission of the copyright owner. We disclaim any liability
to any person or party for any loss resulting from reliance on
information within this book.

Color the girls hair, eyes, eyebrows, lips and the clothes they wear with colored pencils and add
shading or add sparkling accents with glitter gel pens. Or color their skin with brown colored pencil to look like a fake tan.

You can add a background for each of the girl's portrait and shade it. Rosa's rectangular background serves as a guide for the other girl's portrait. And you can write descriptions for each of the girl's portrait.

You can rename their group and rename each character. Create your favorite character with this coloring book! Have fun with them!

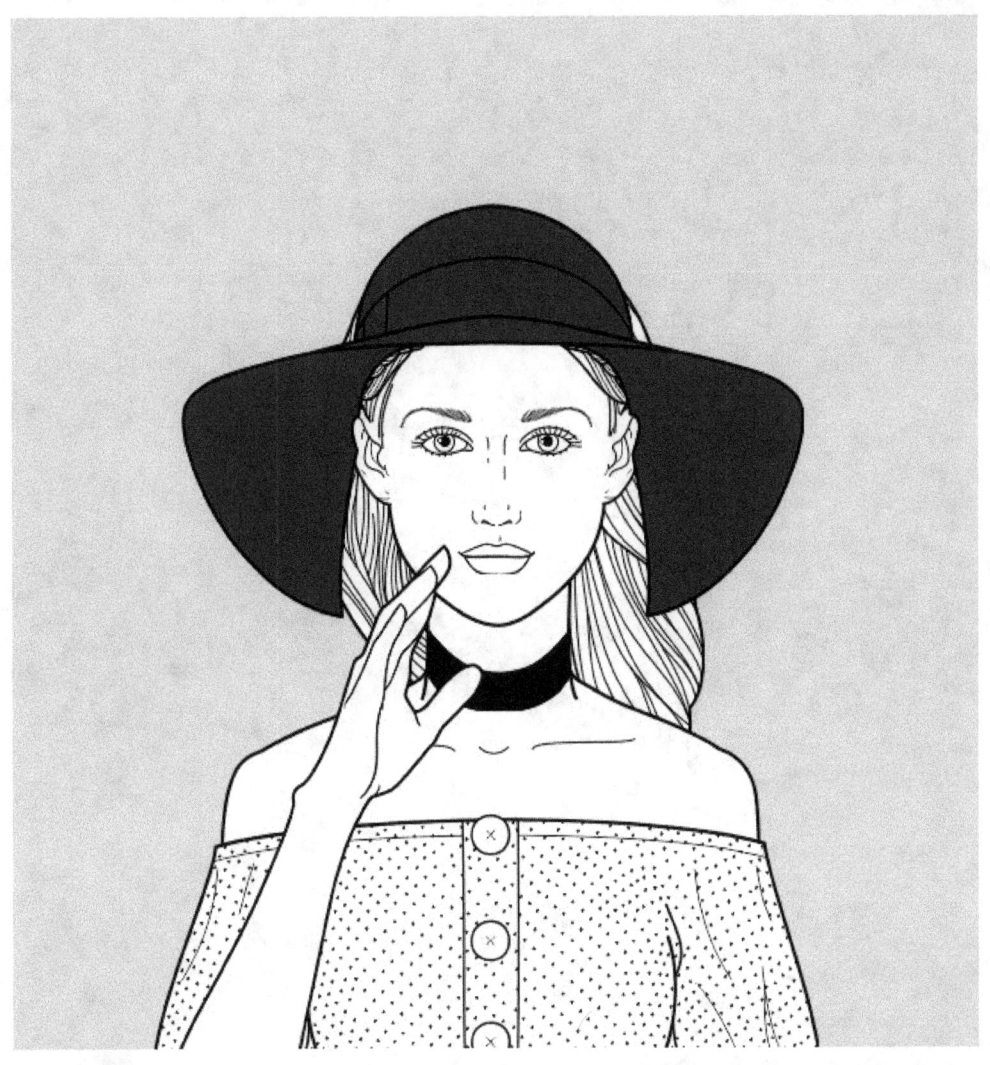

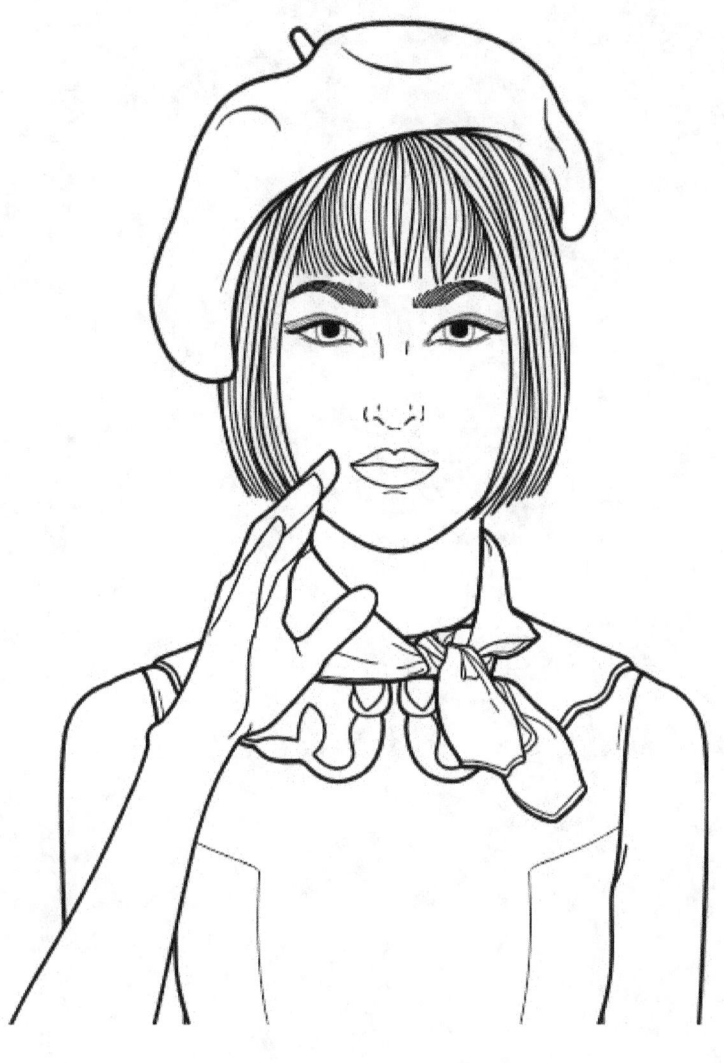

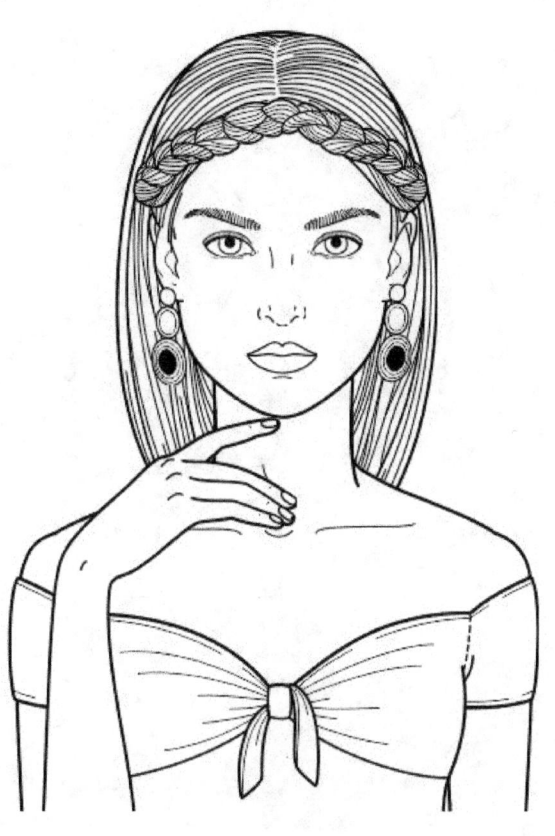

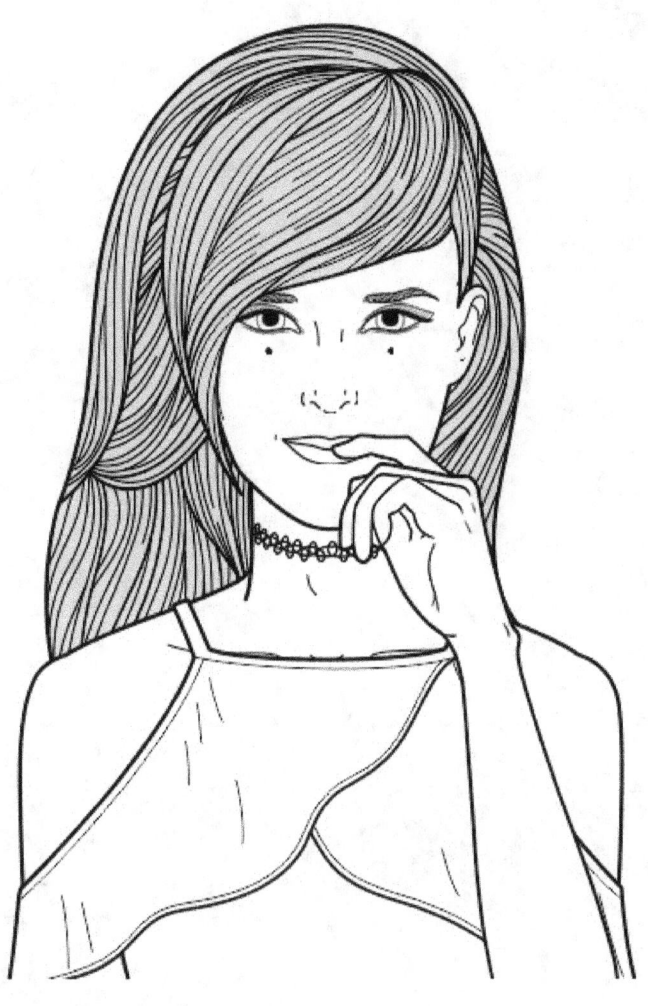

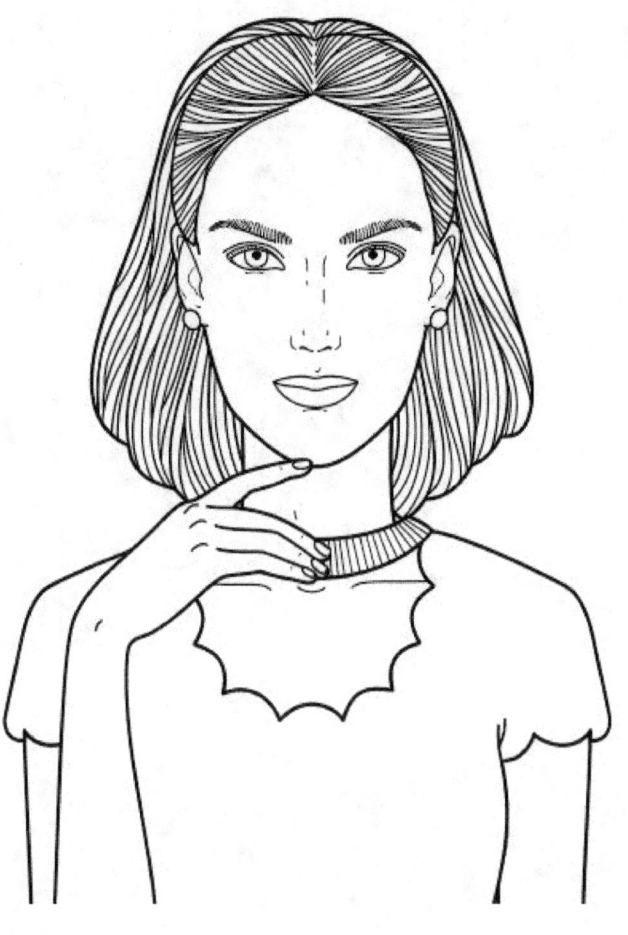

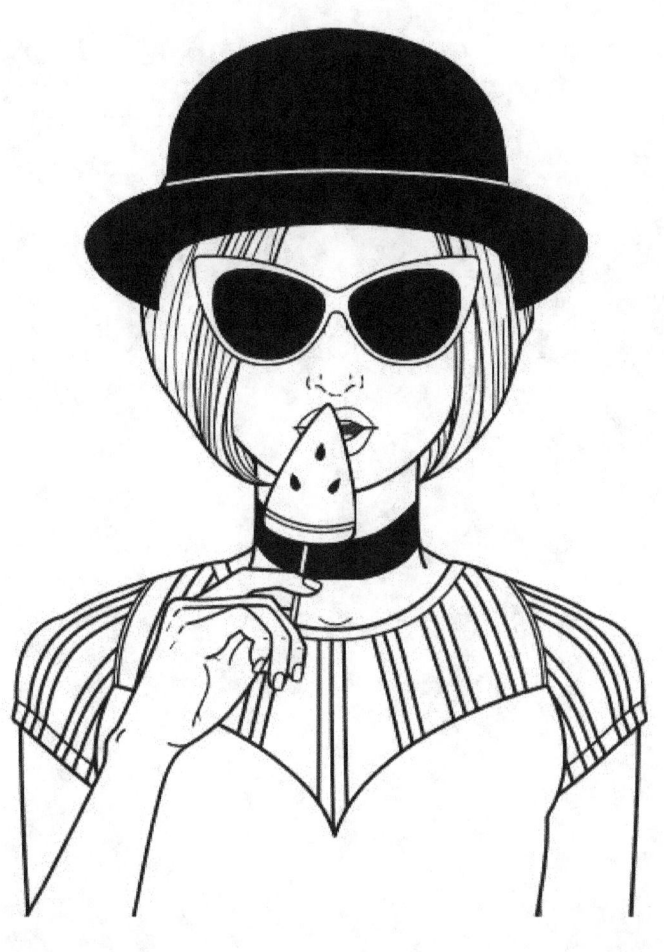

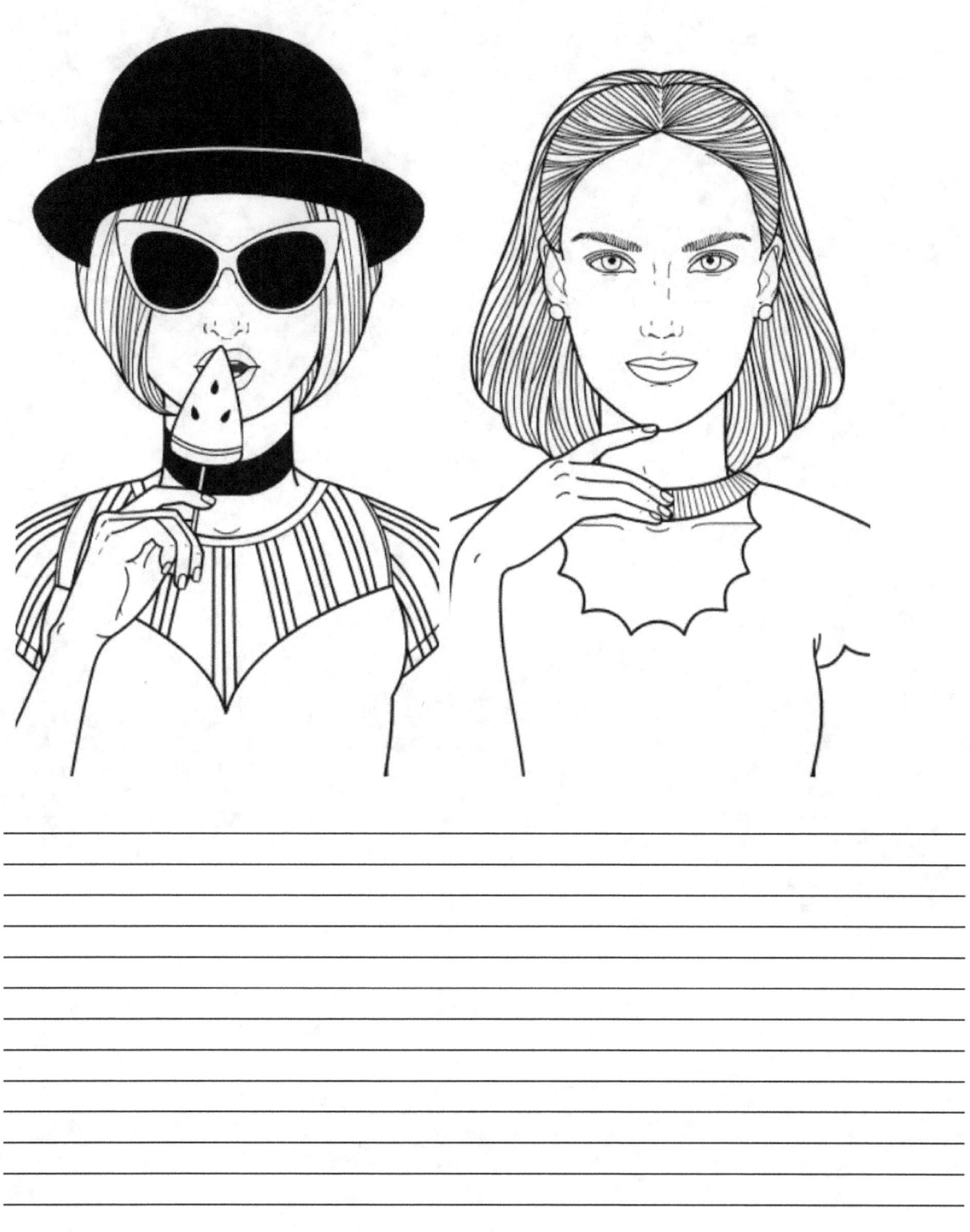

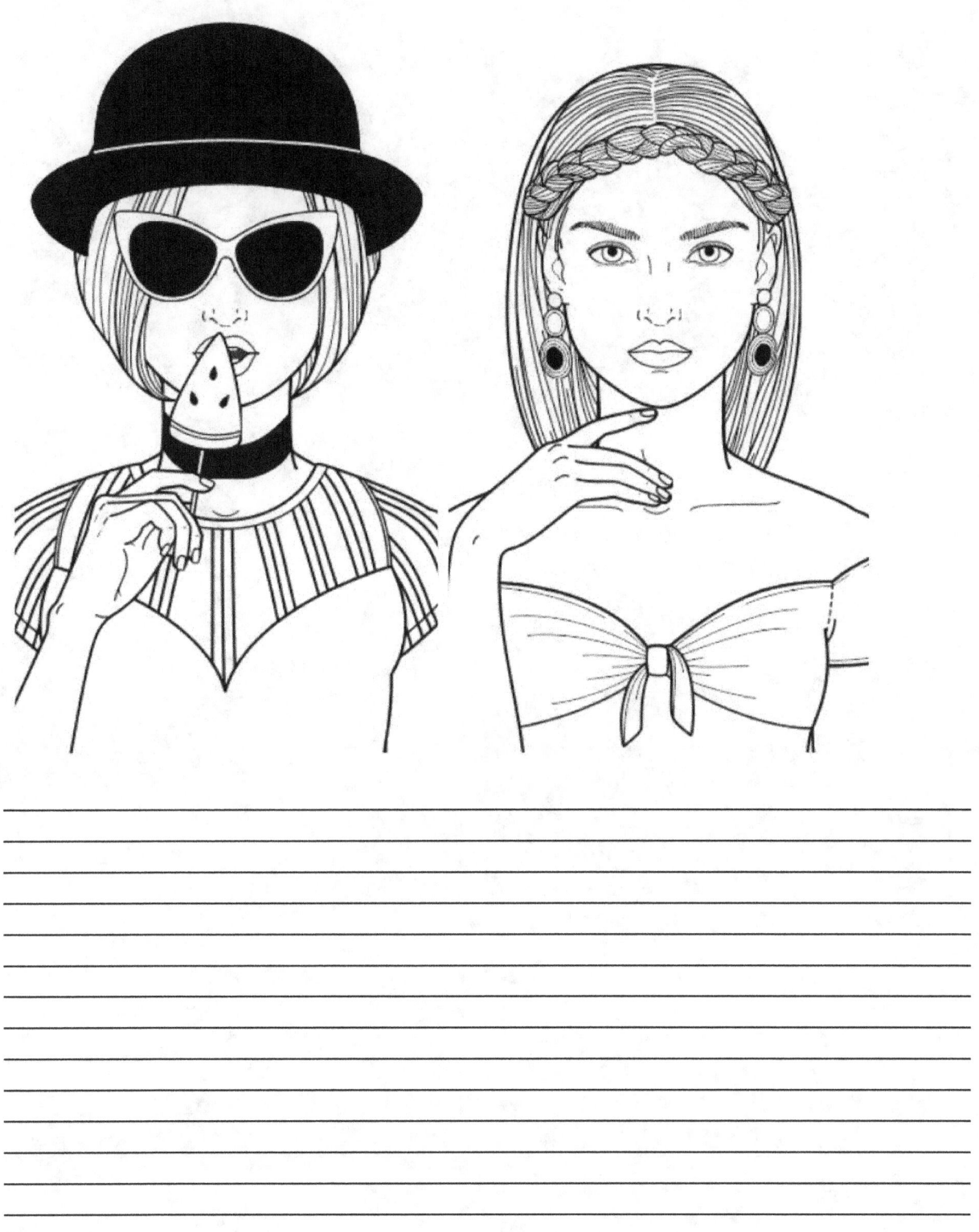

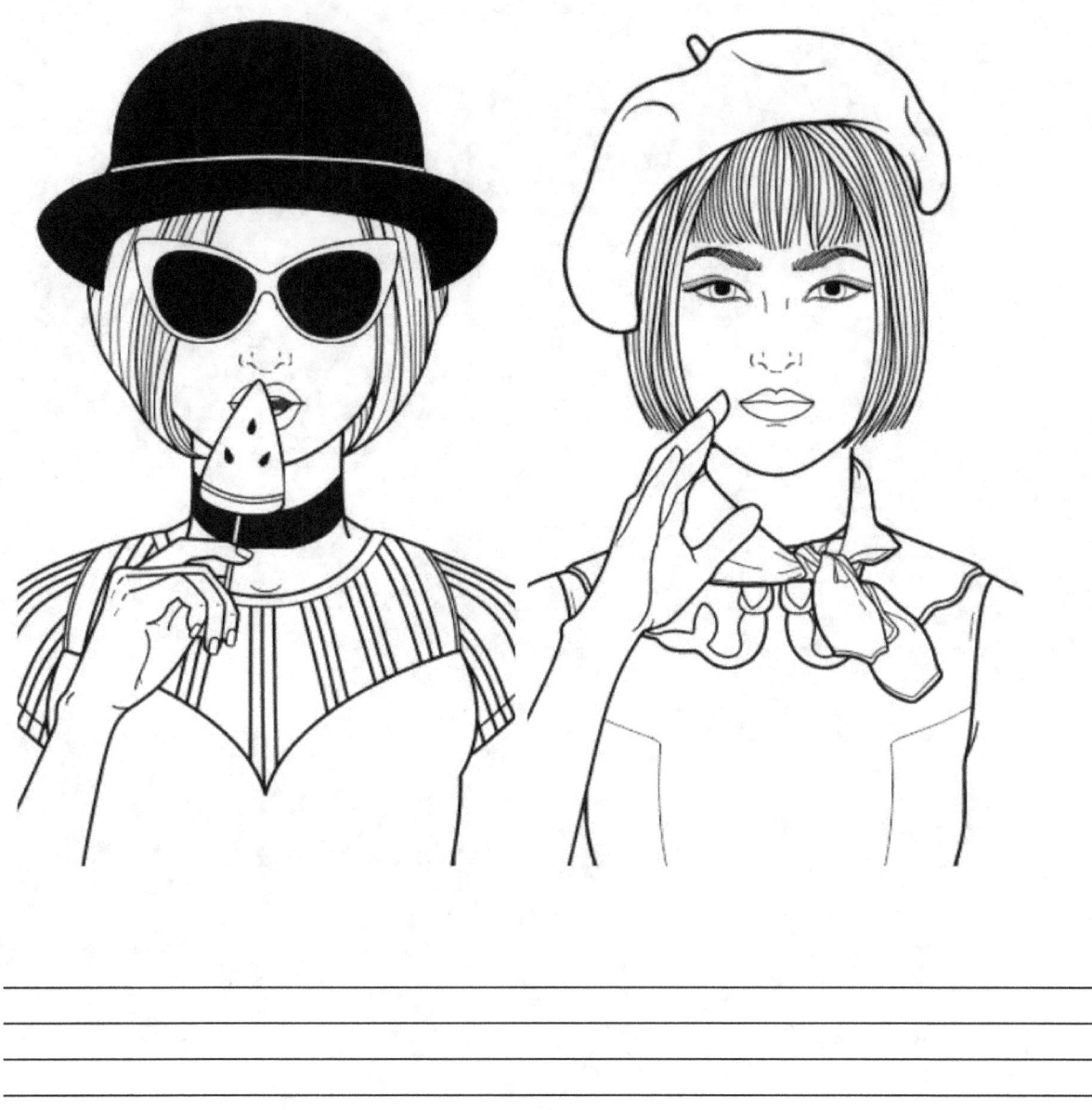

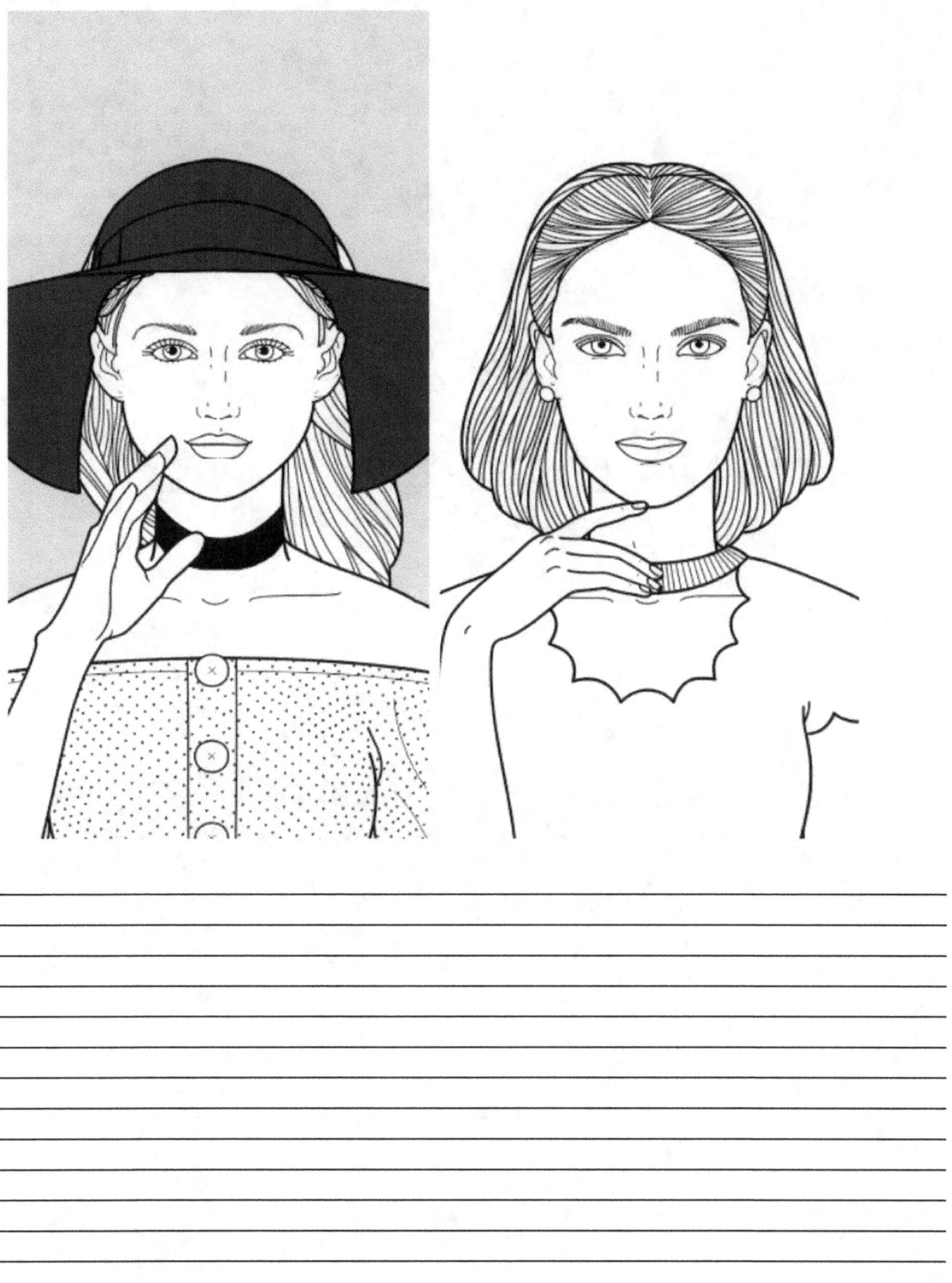

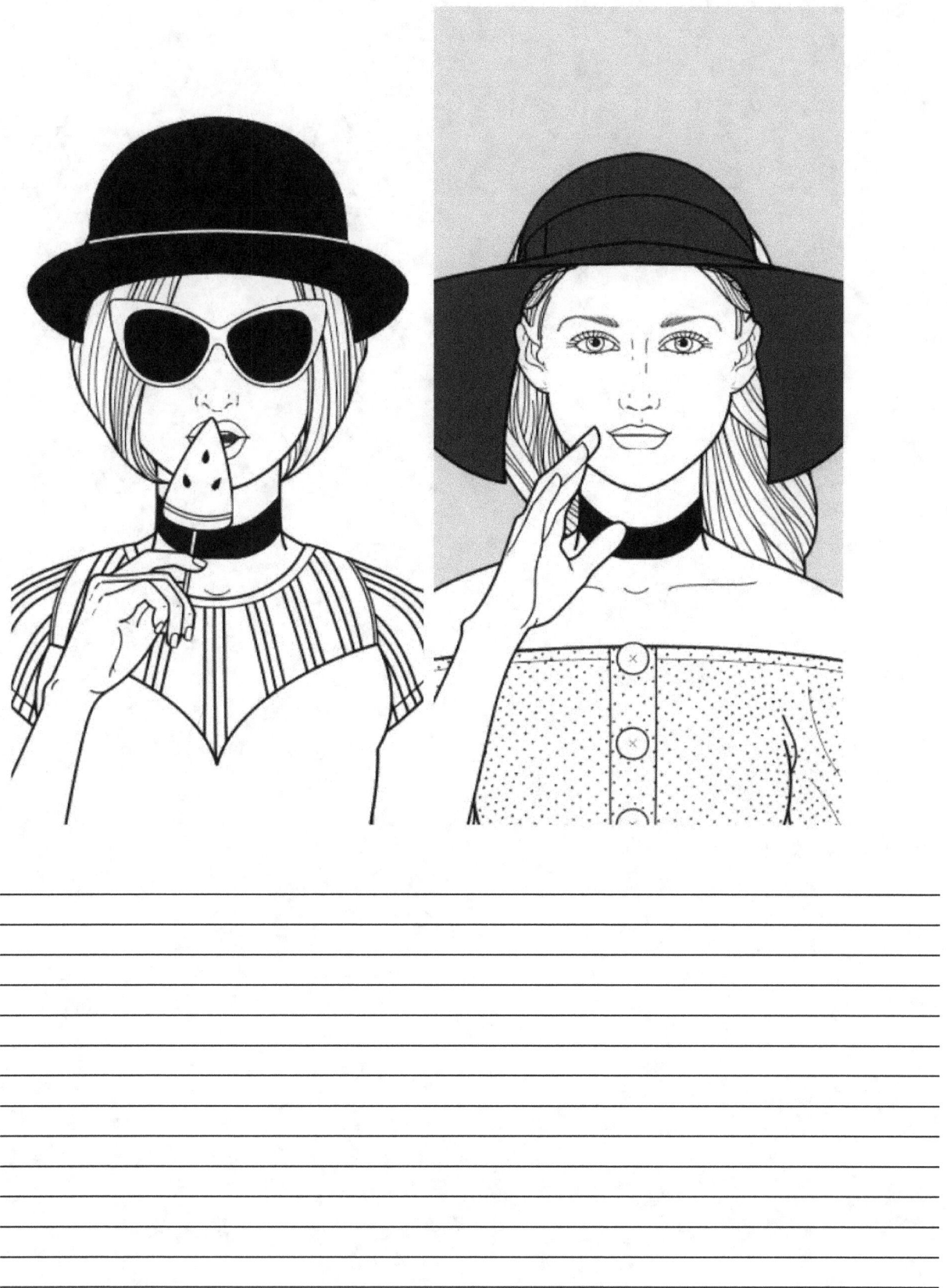

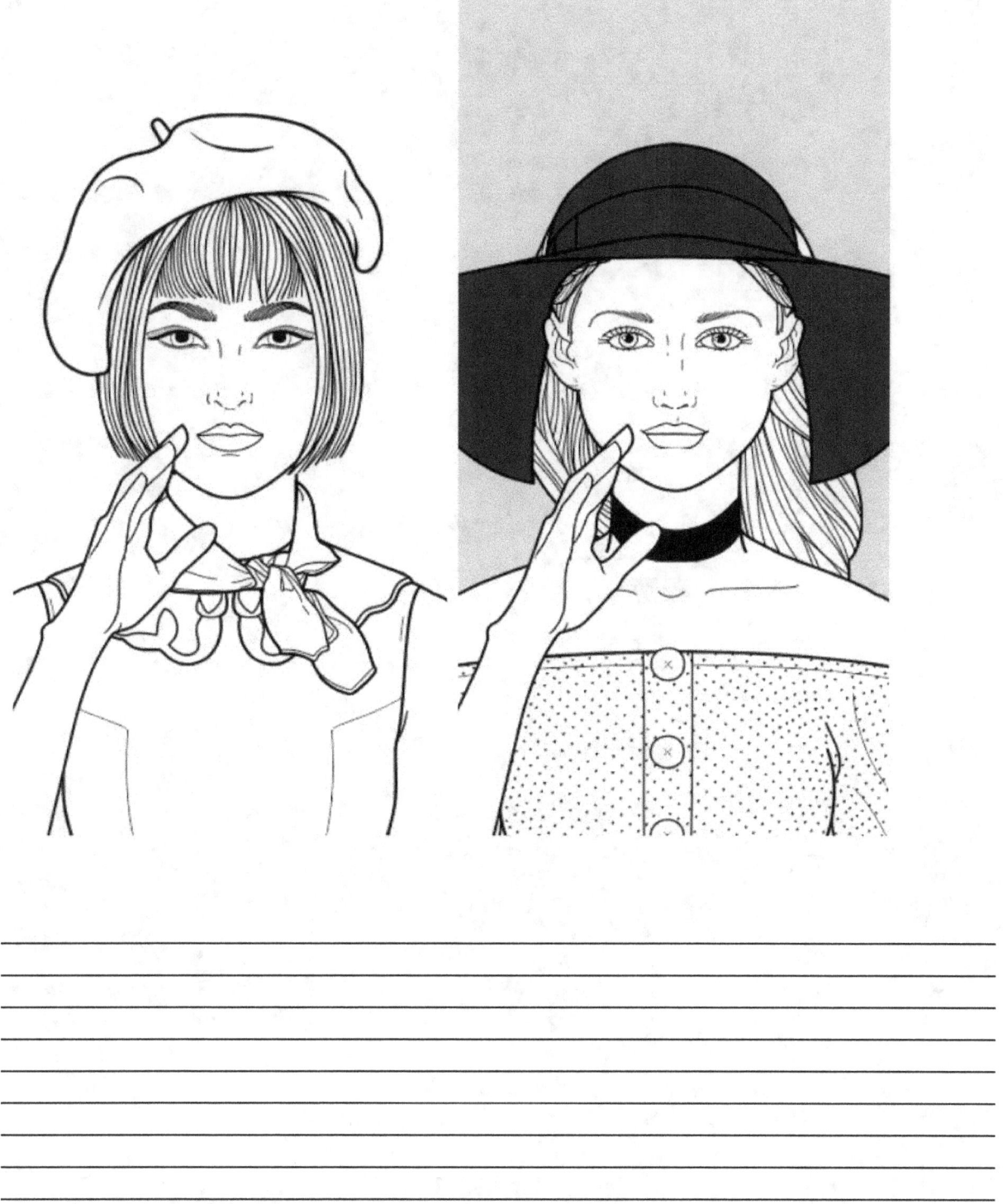

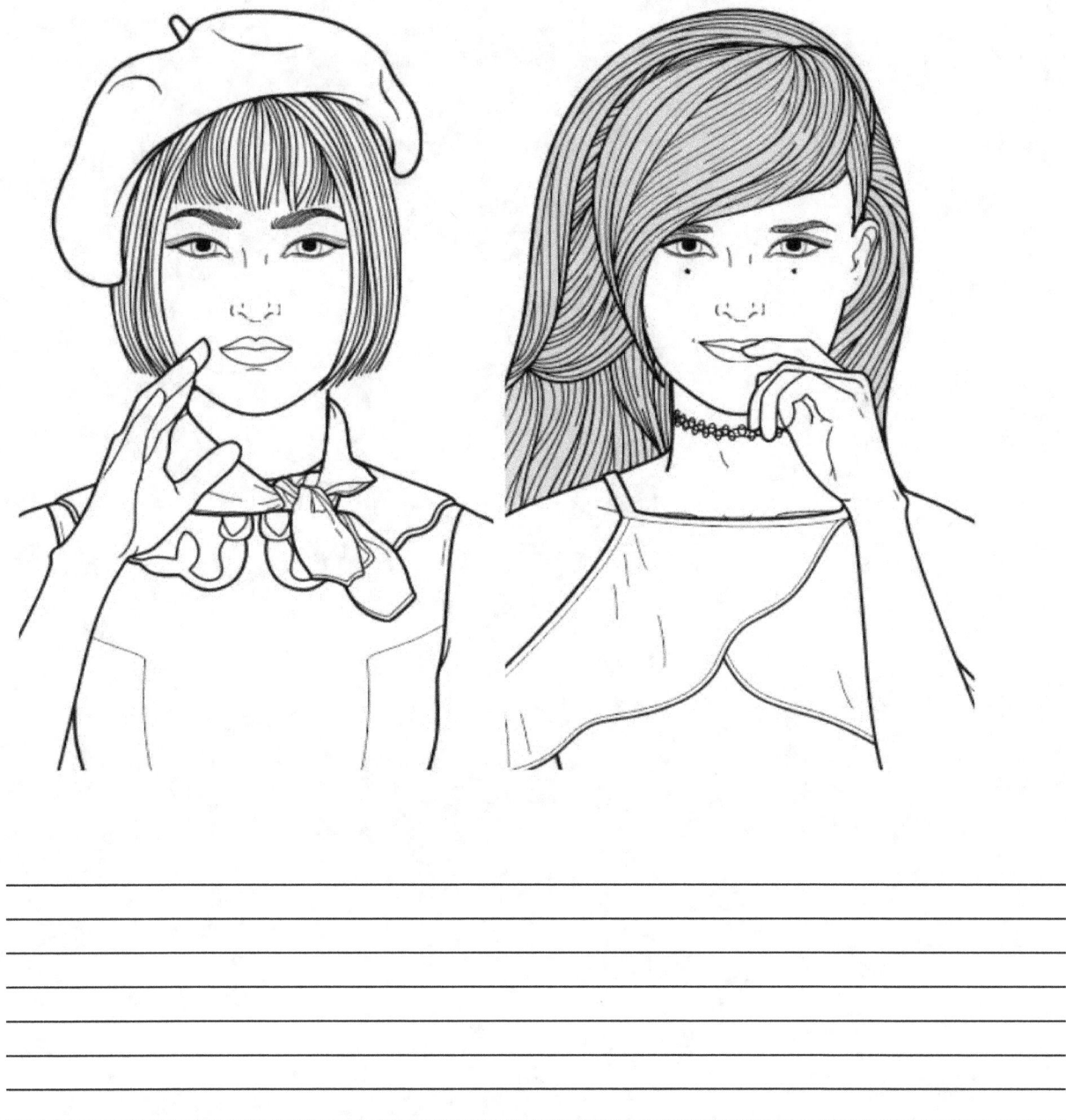

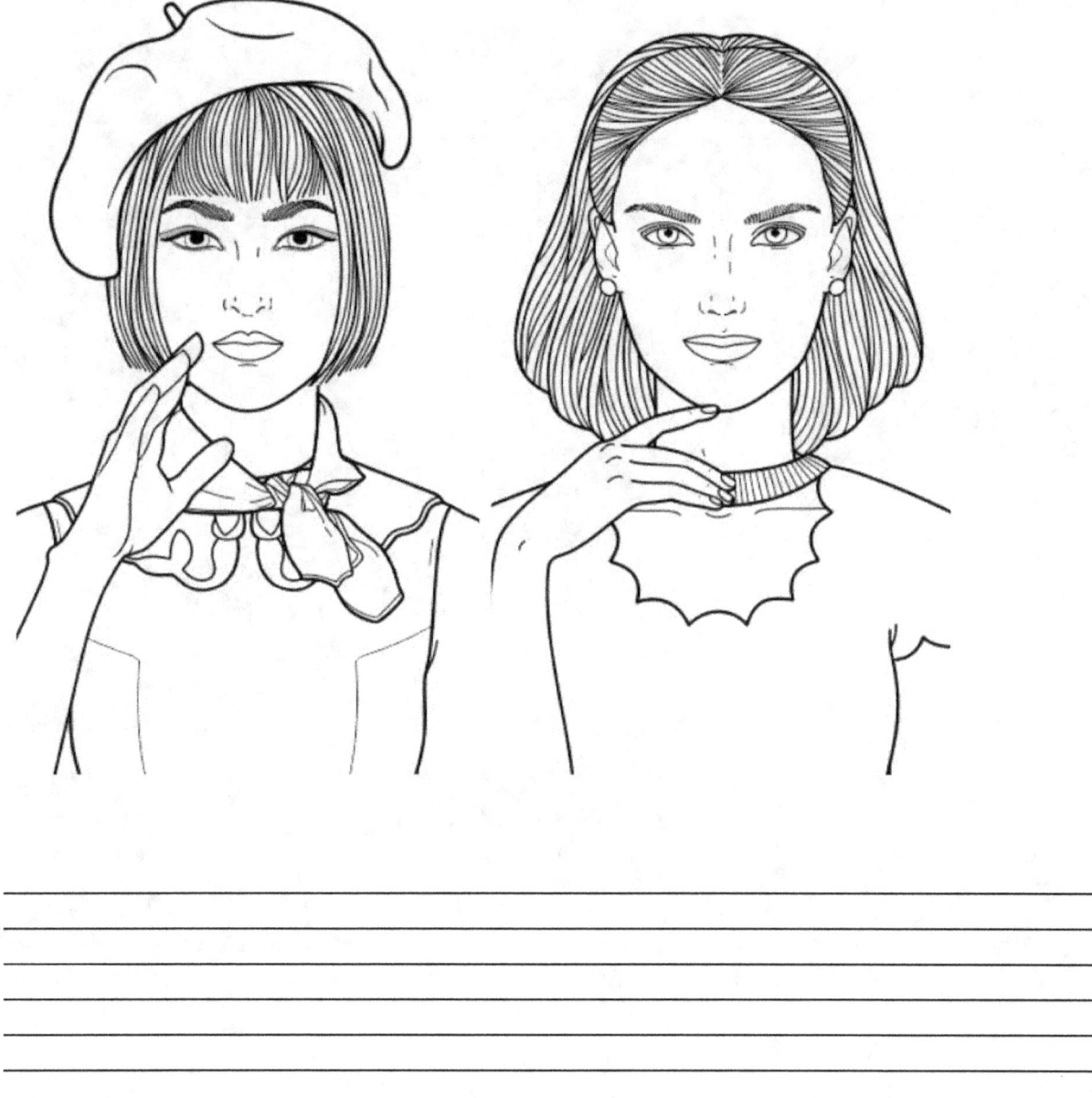

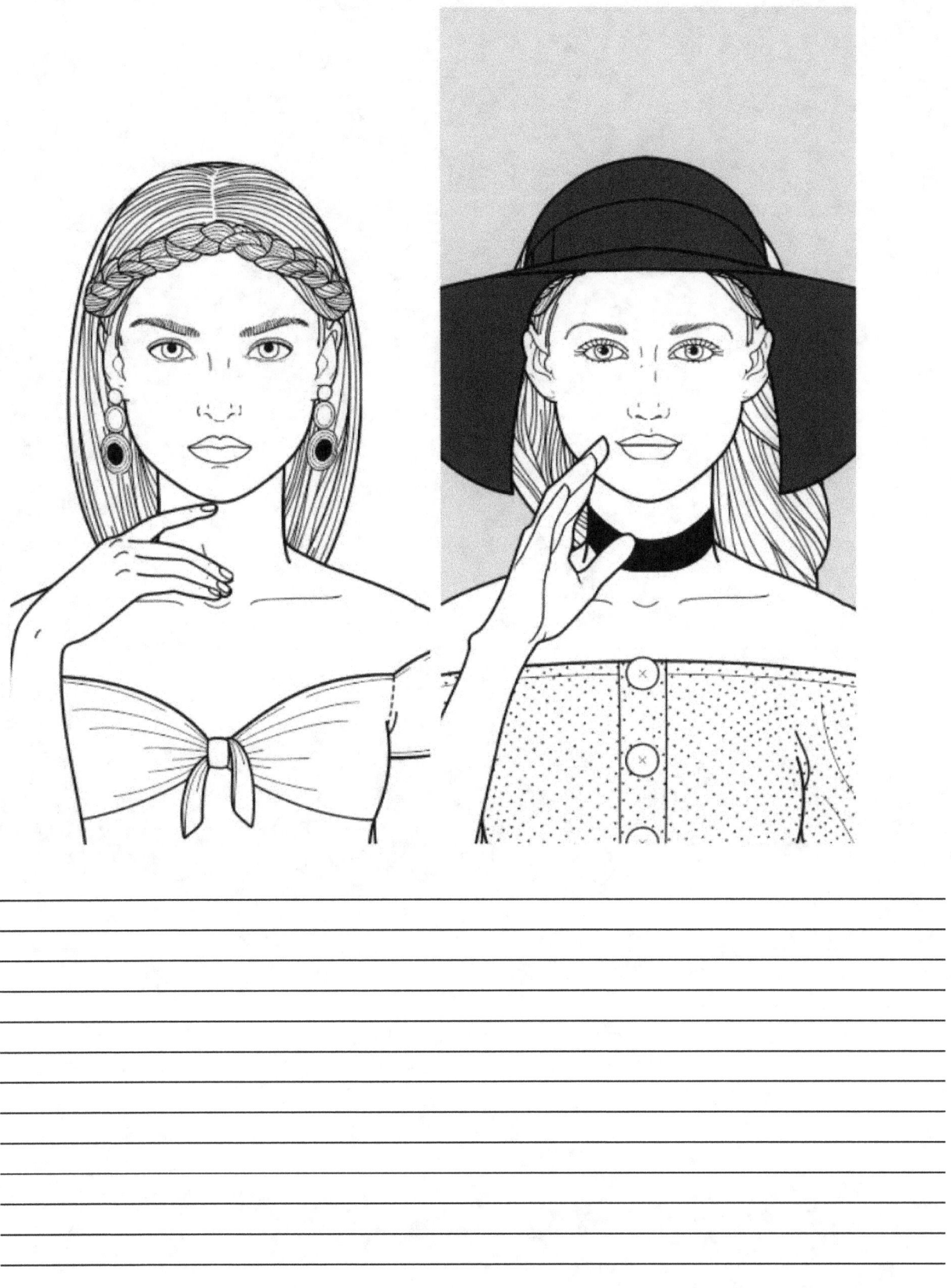

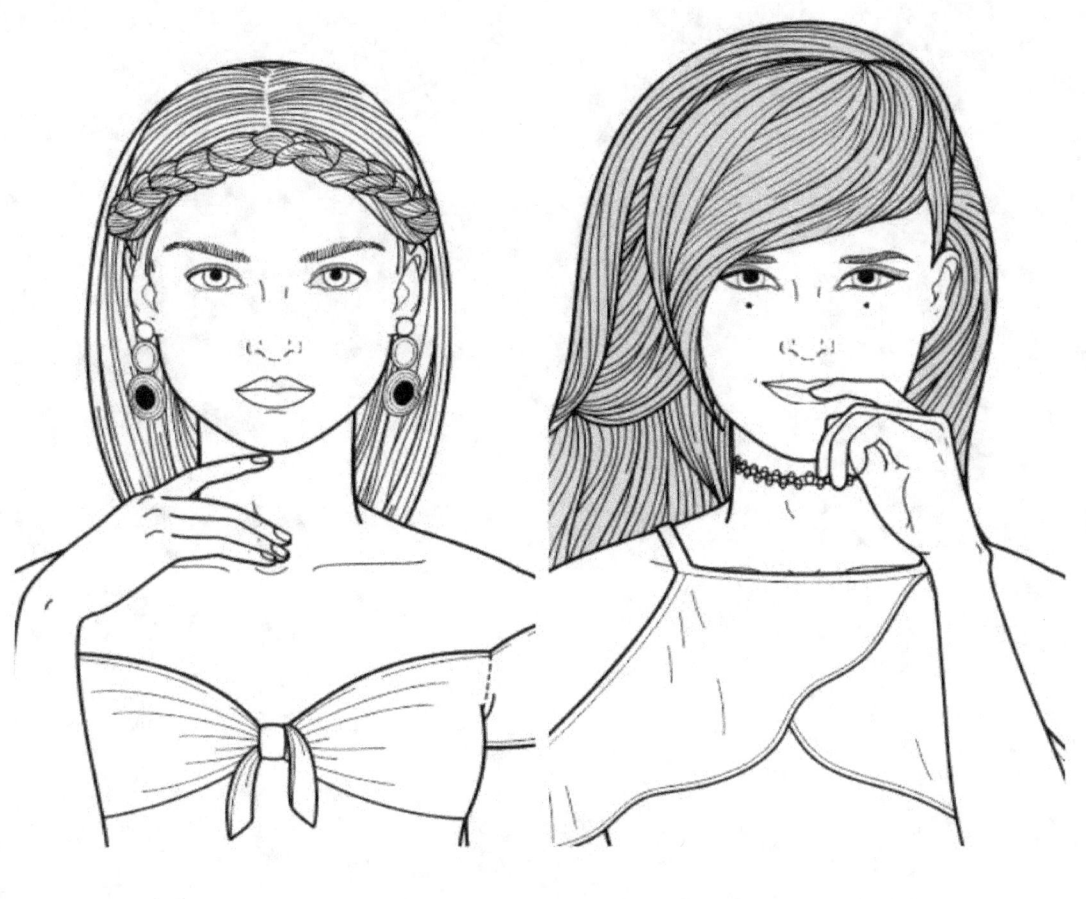

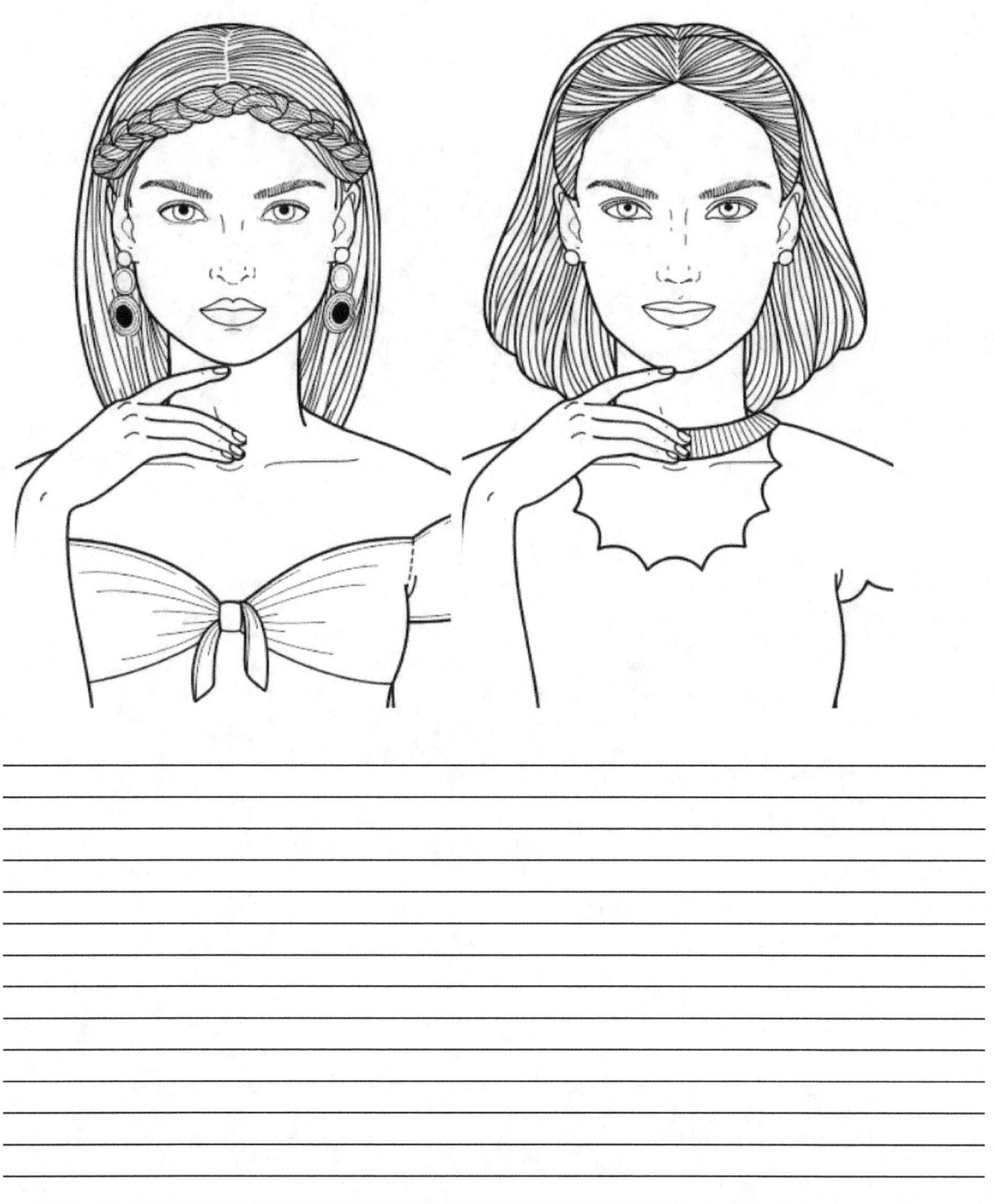

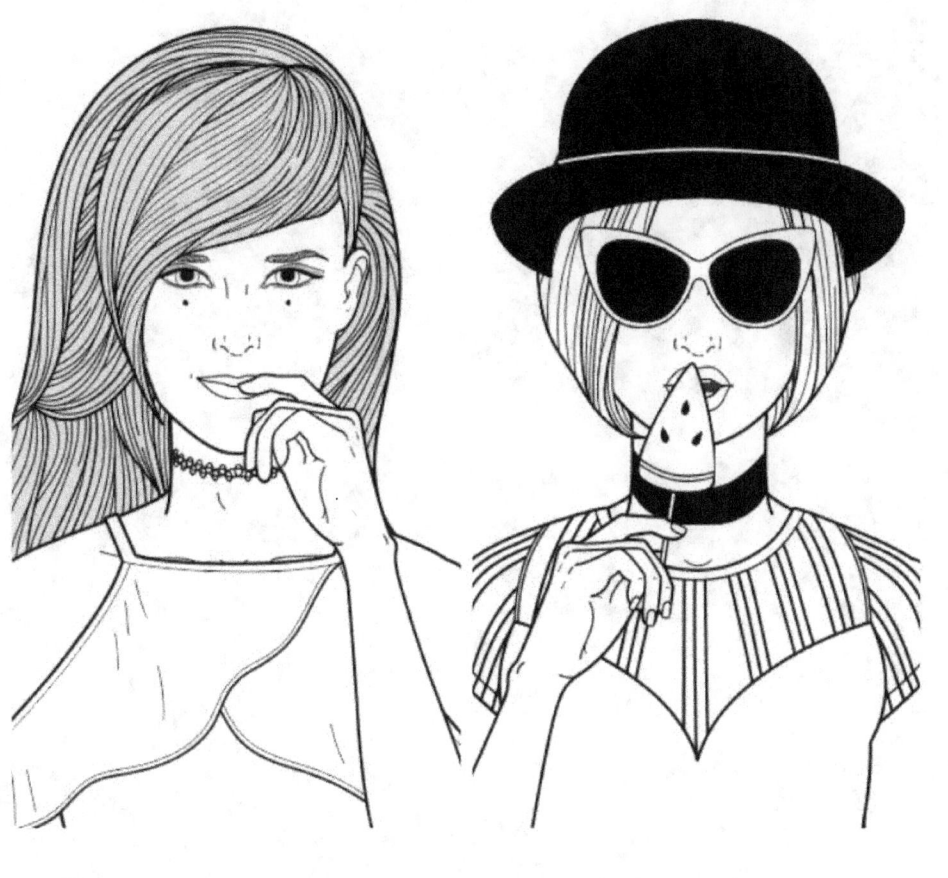

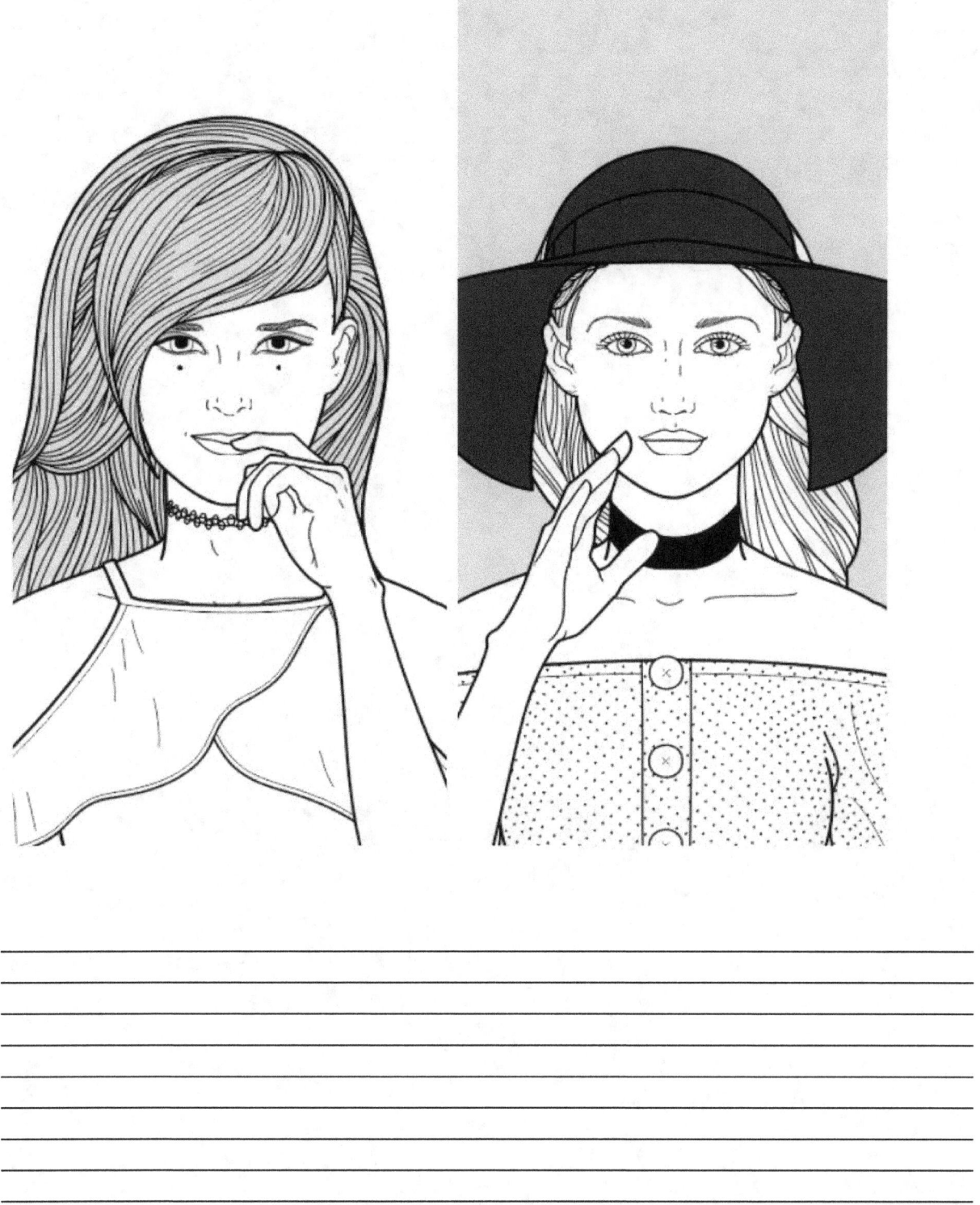

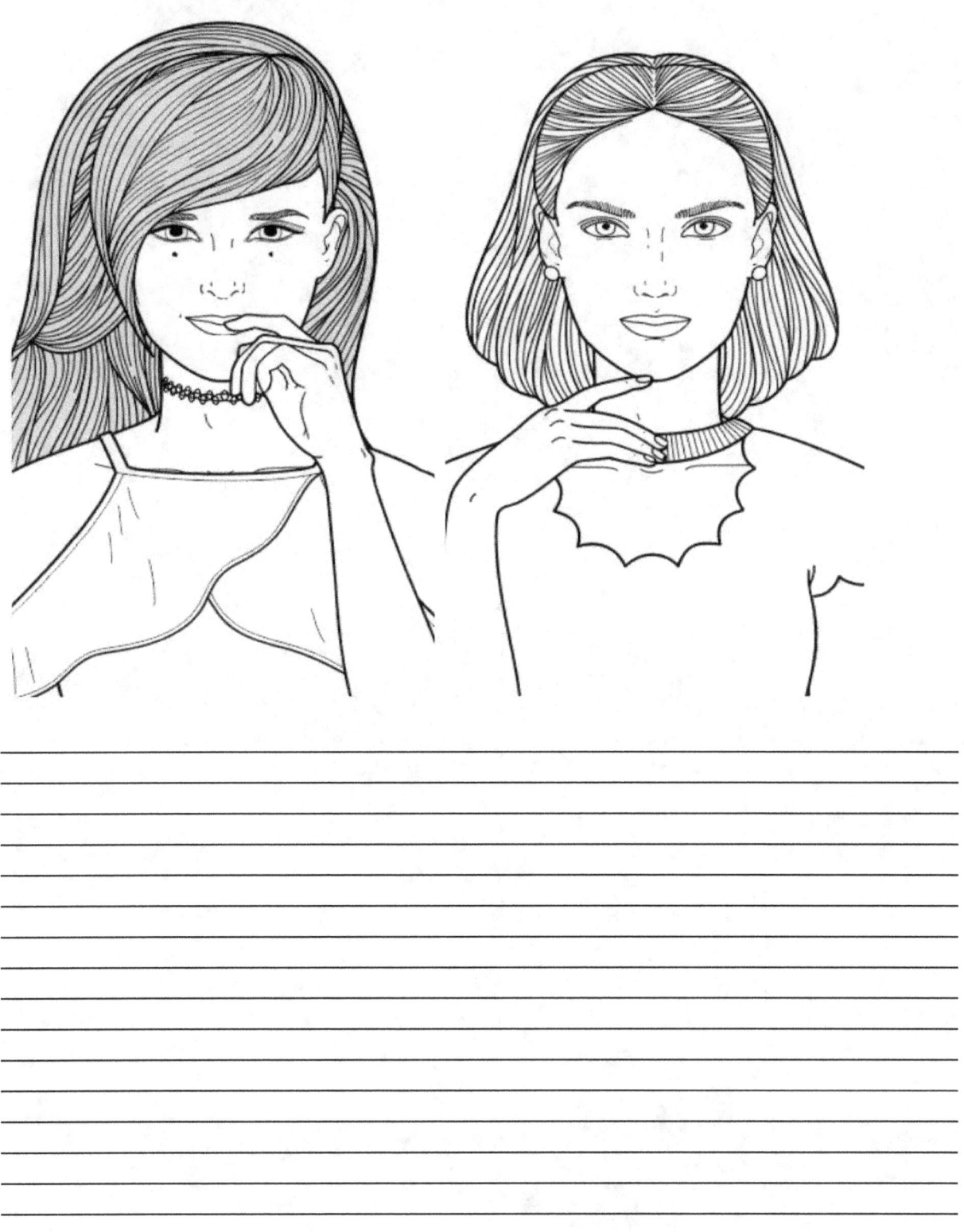

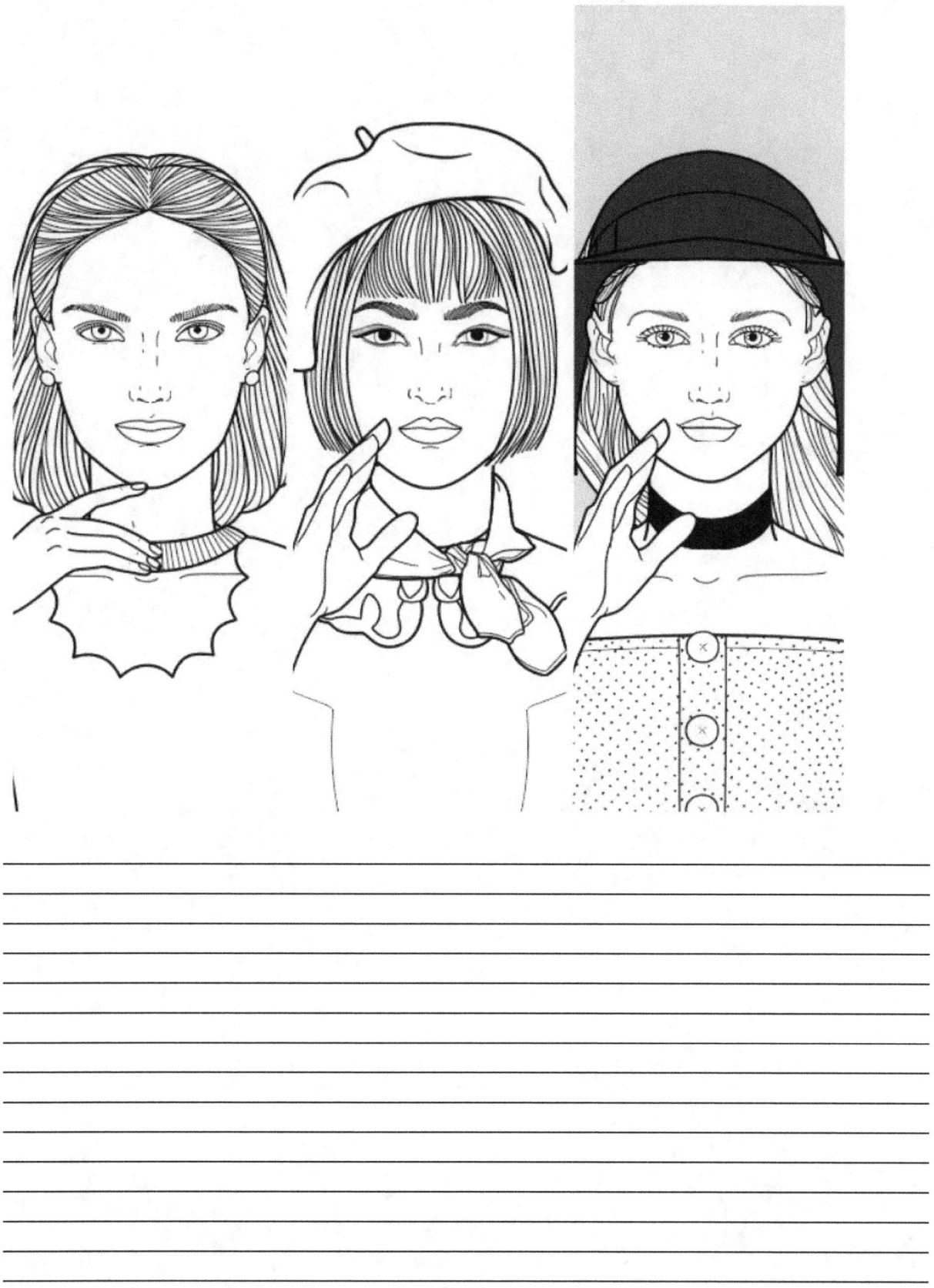

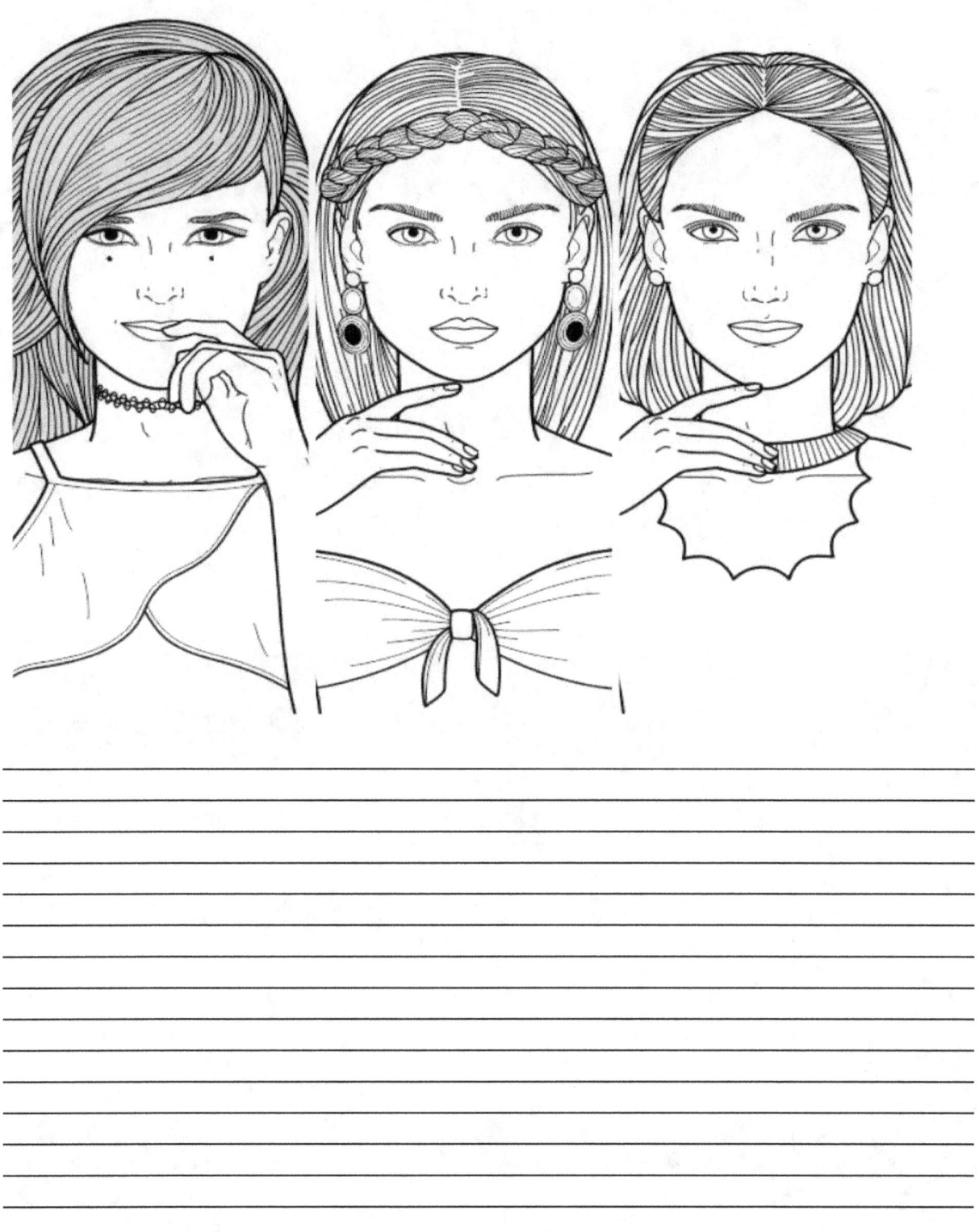

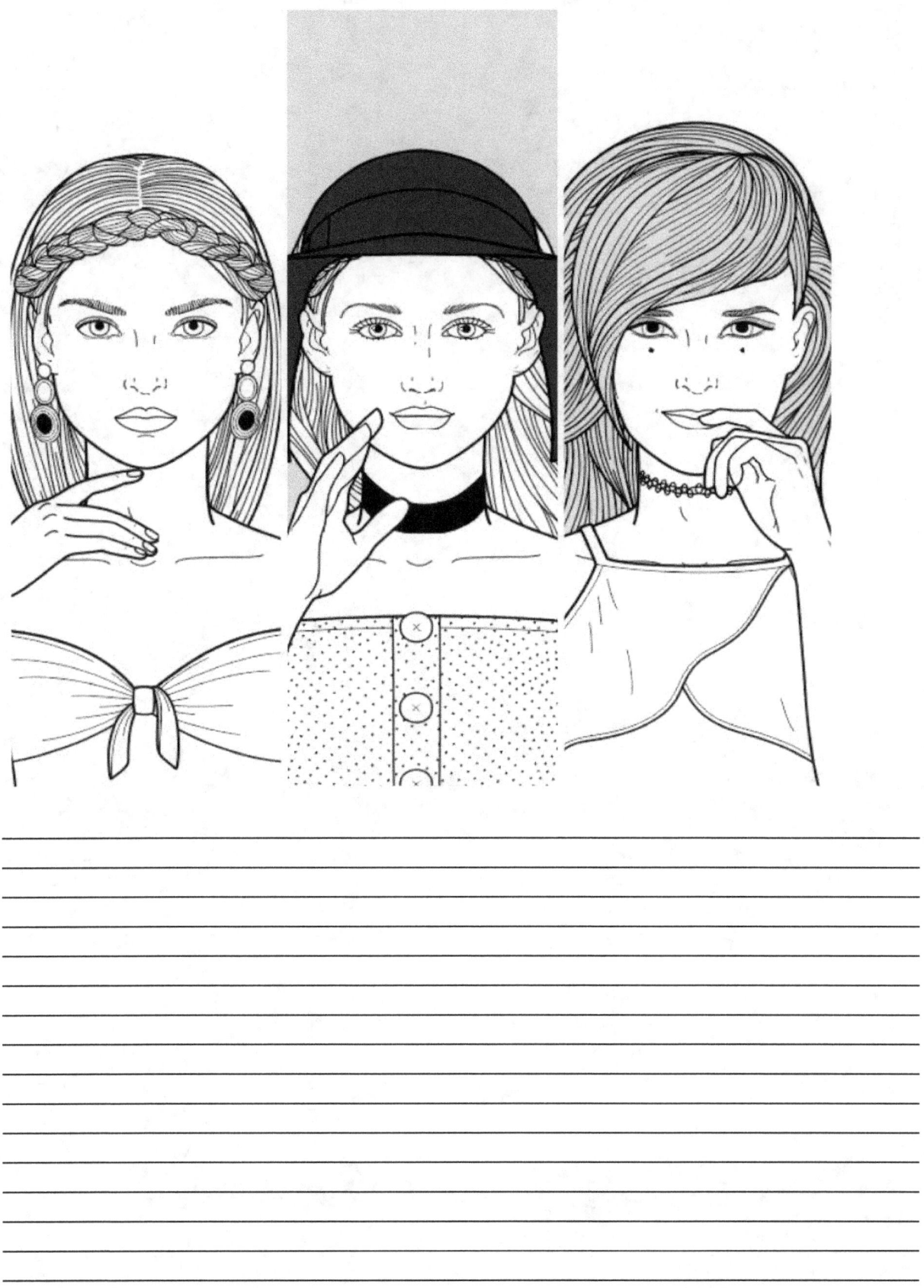

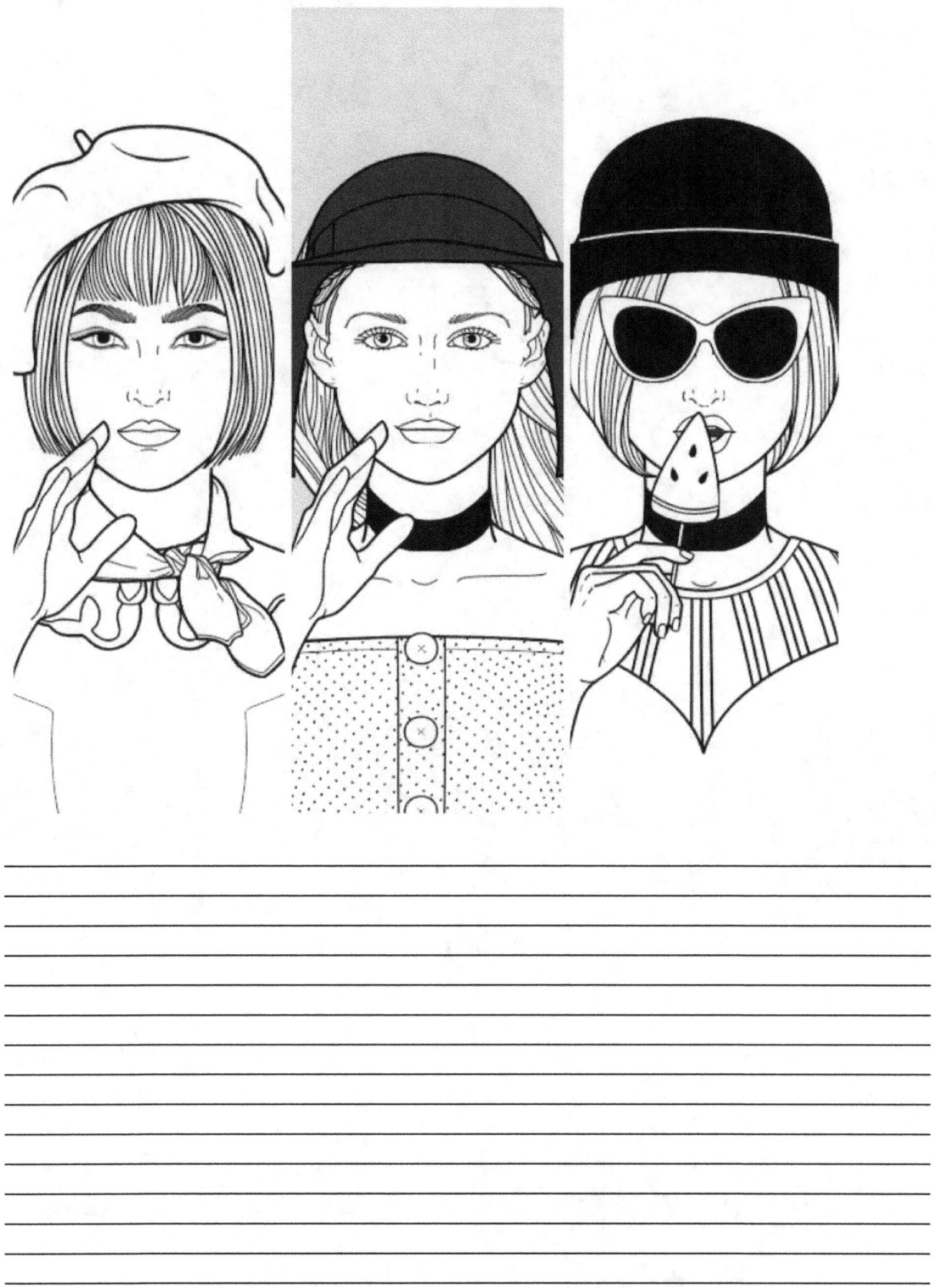

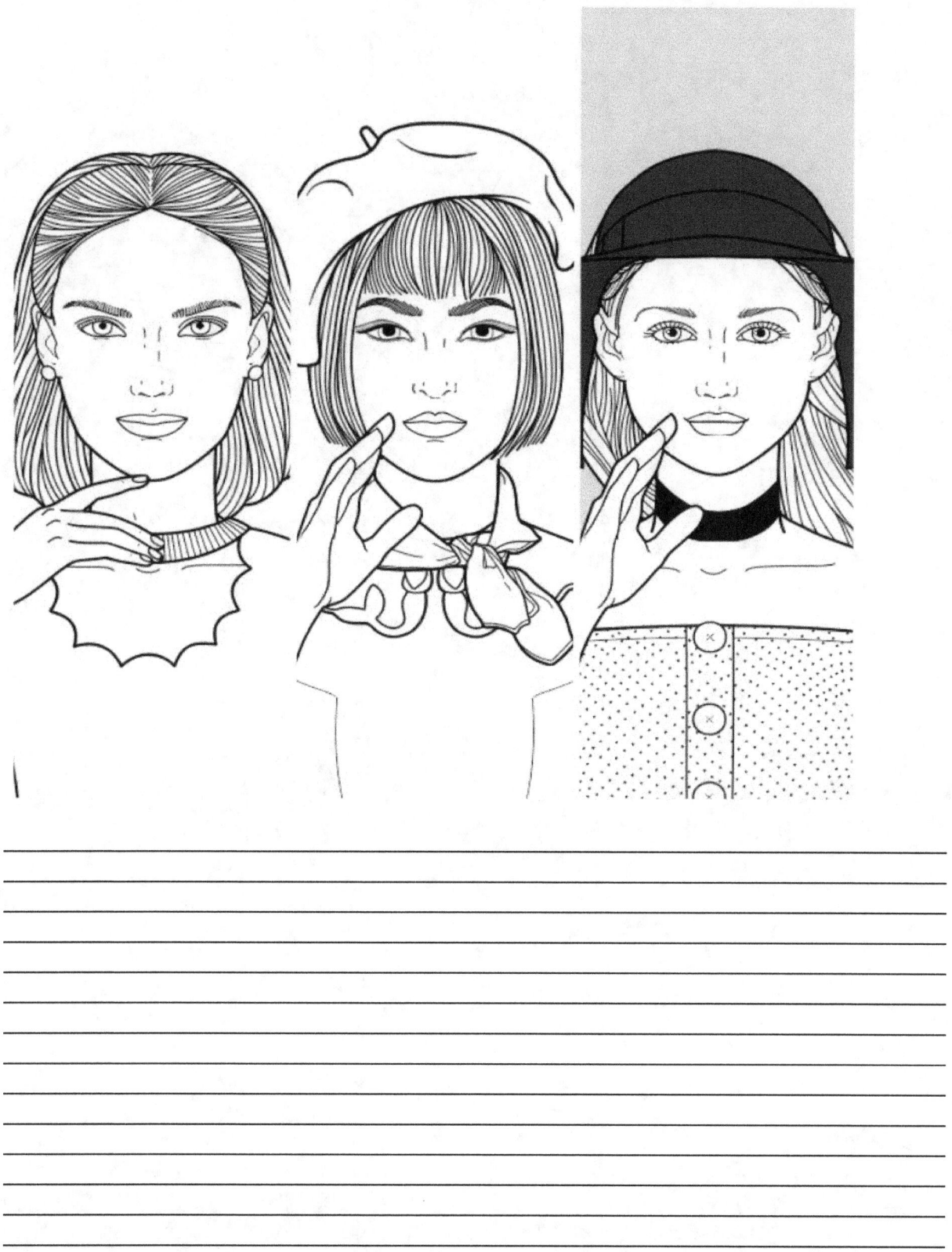

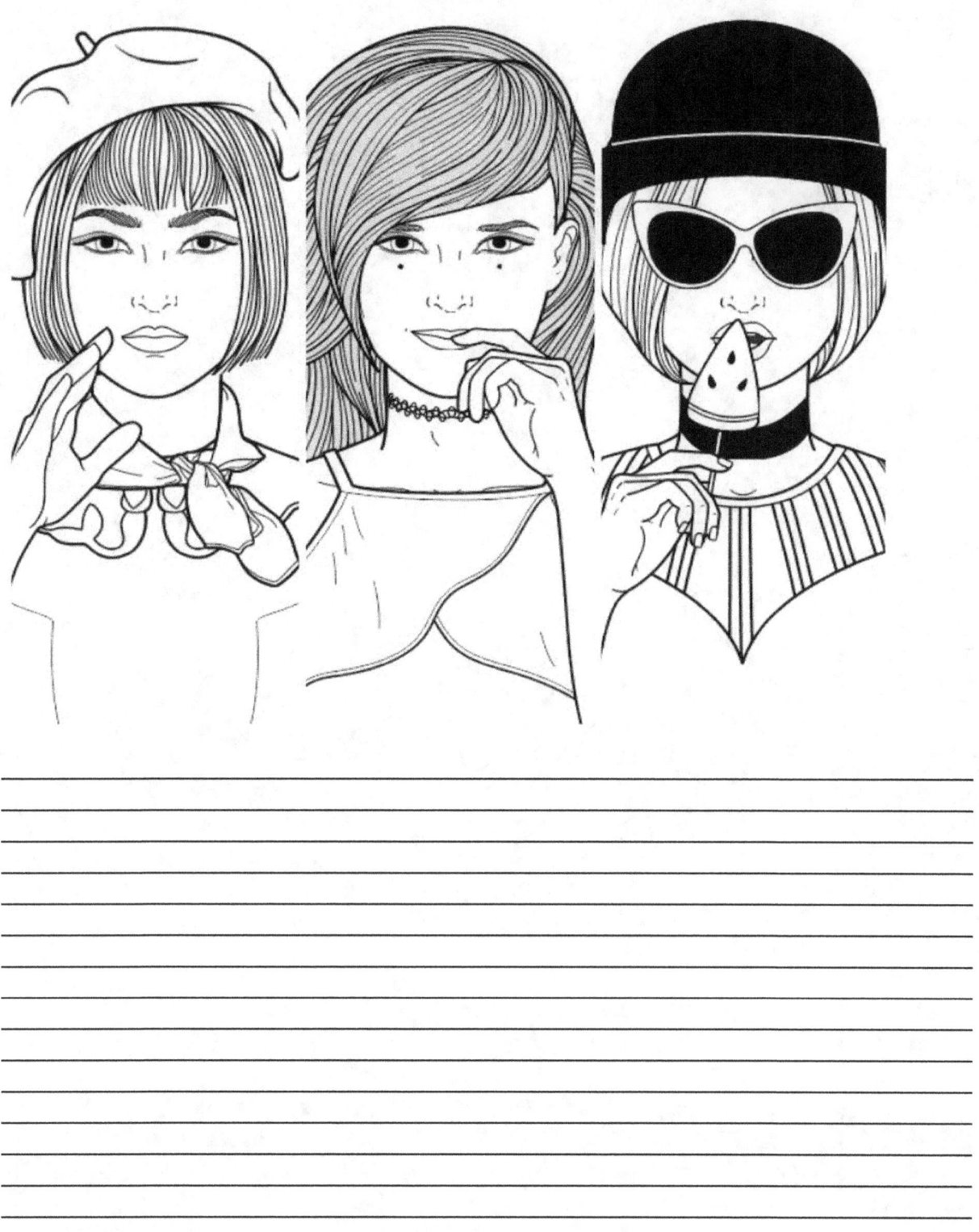

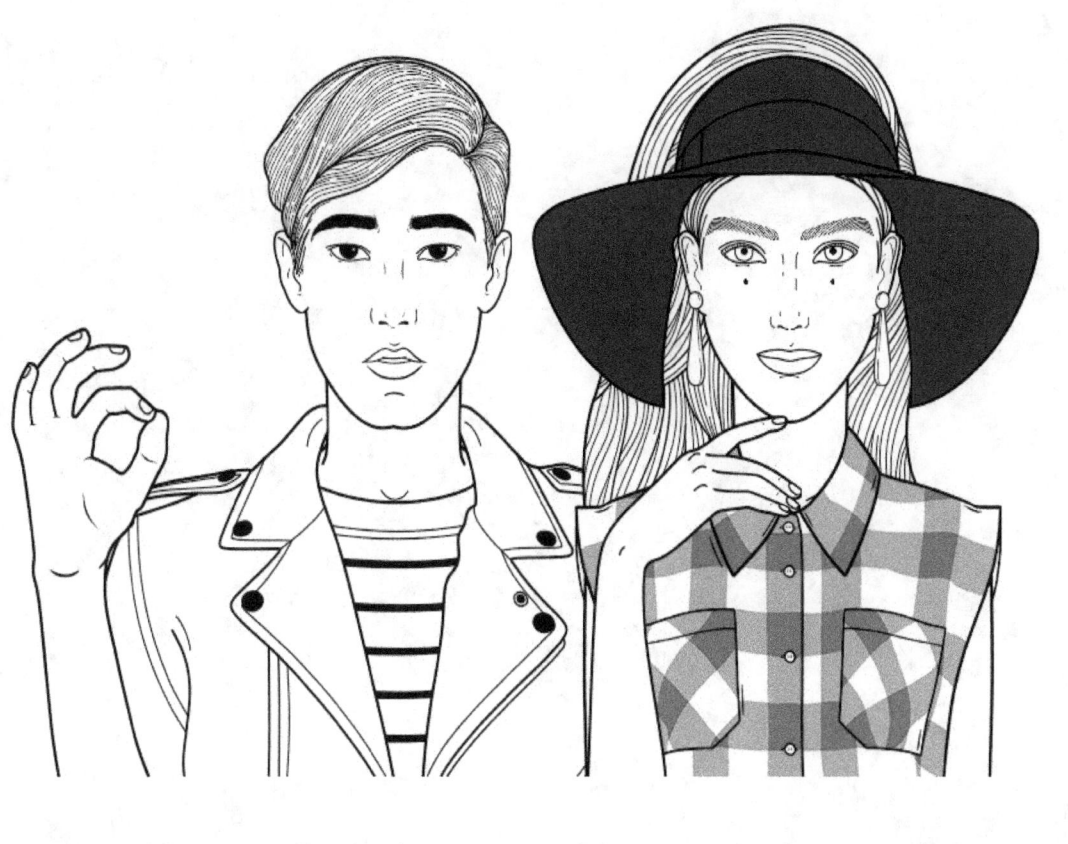

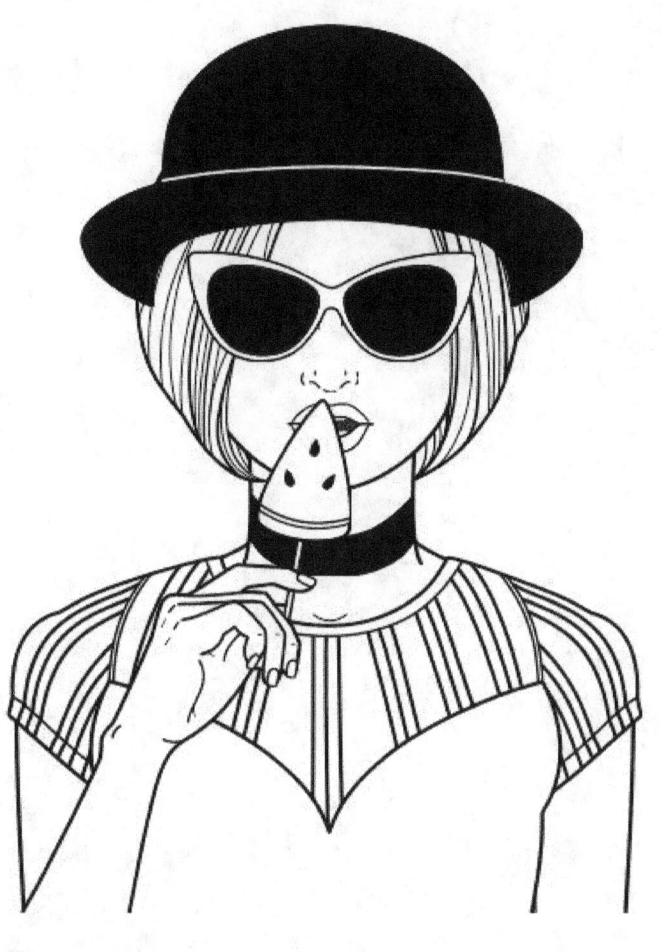

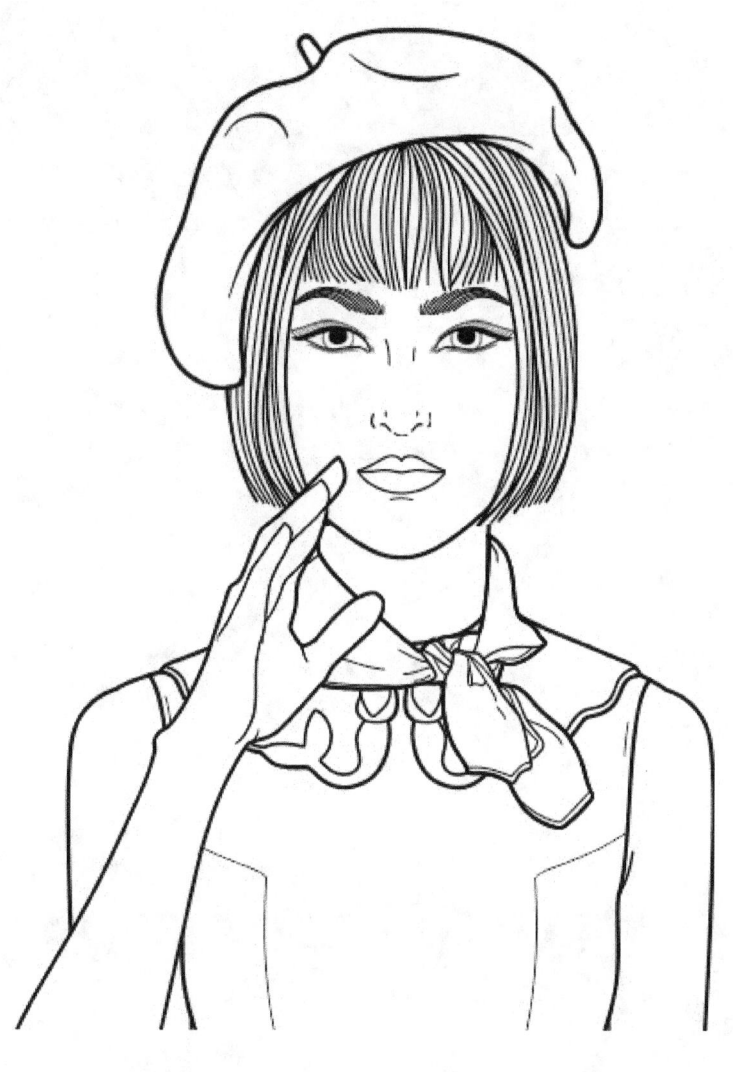

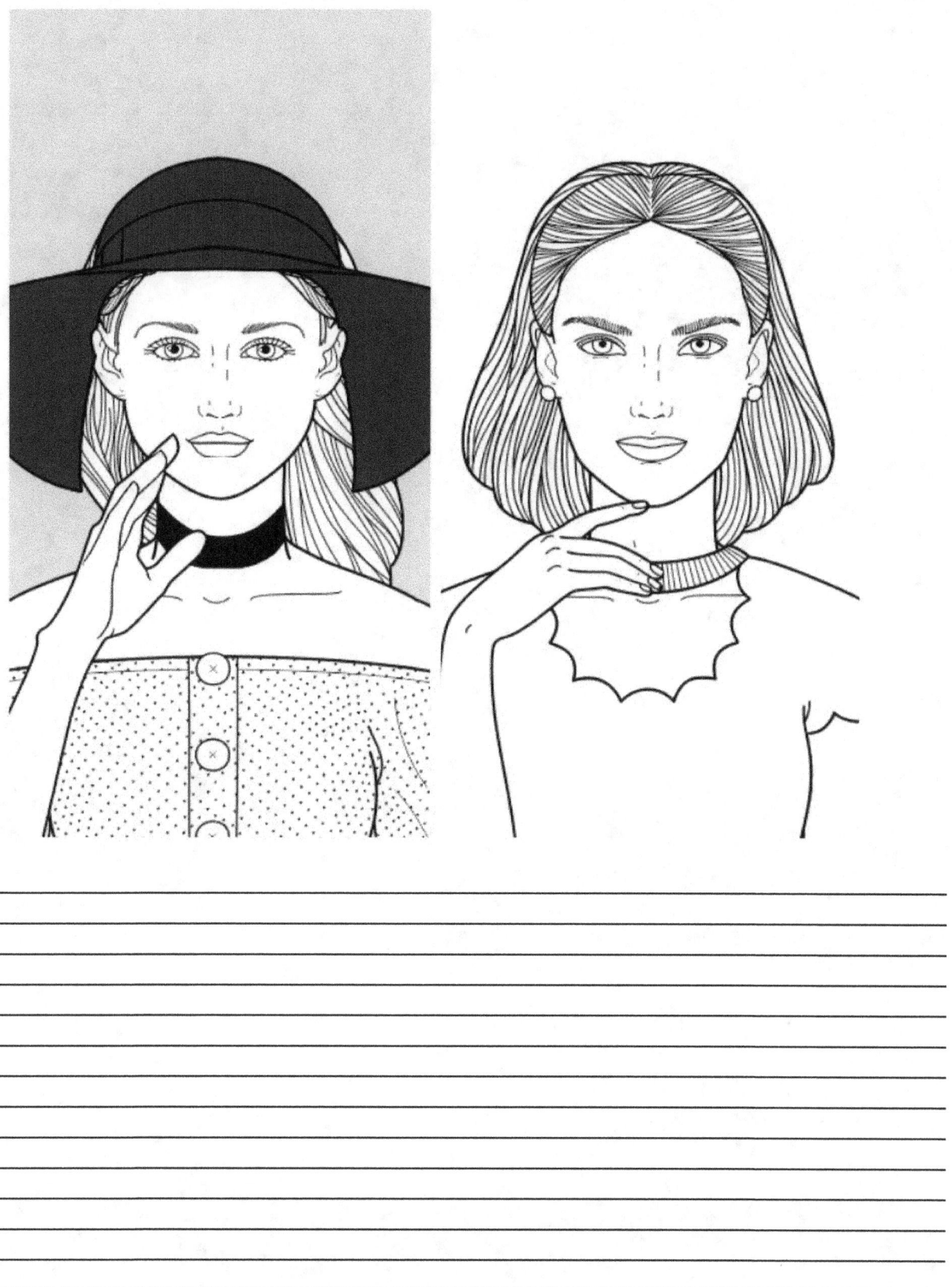

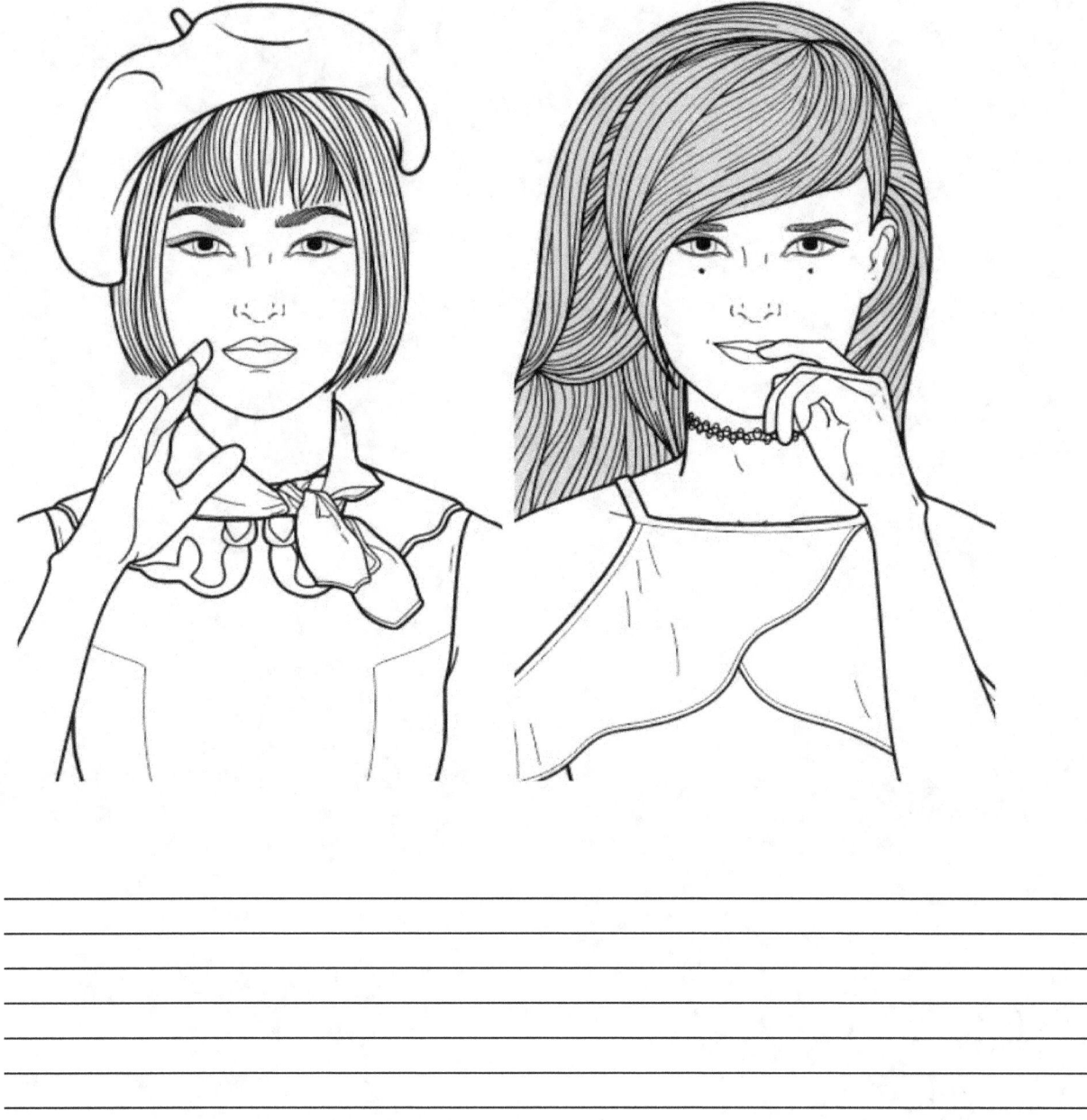

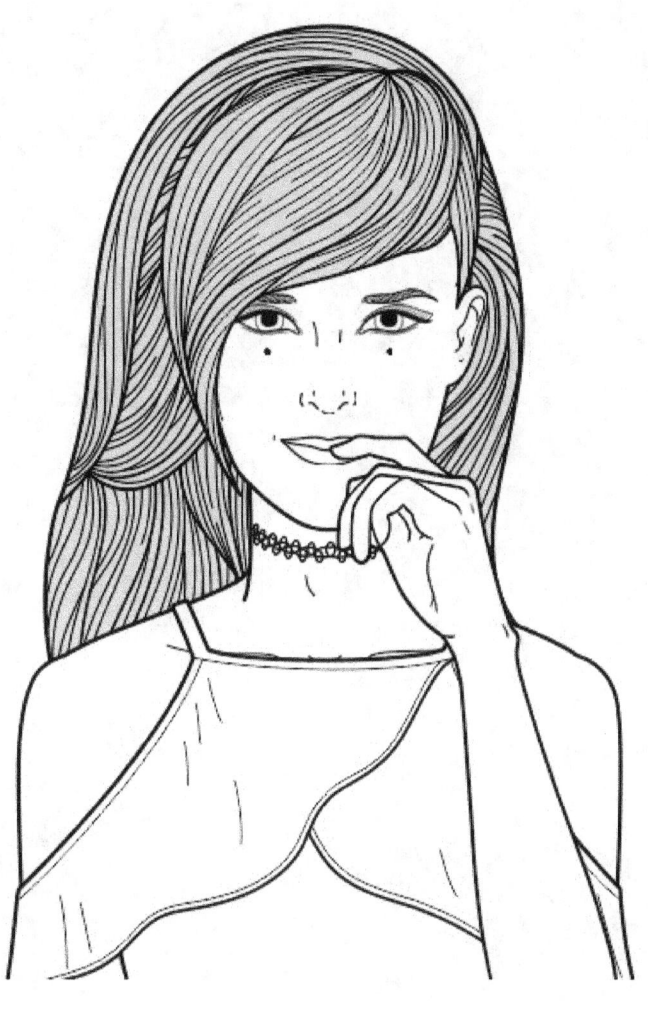

_____
_____
_____
_____
_____
_____
_____
_____

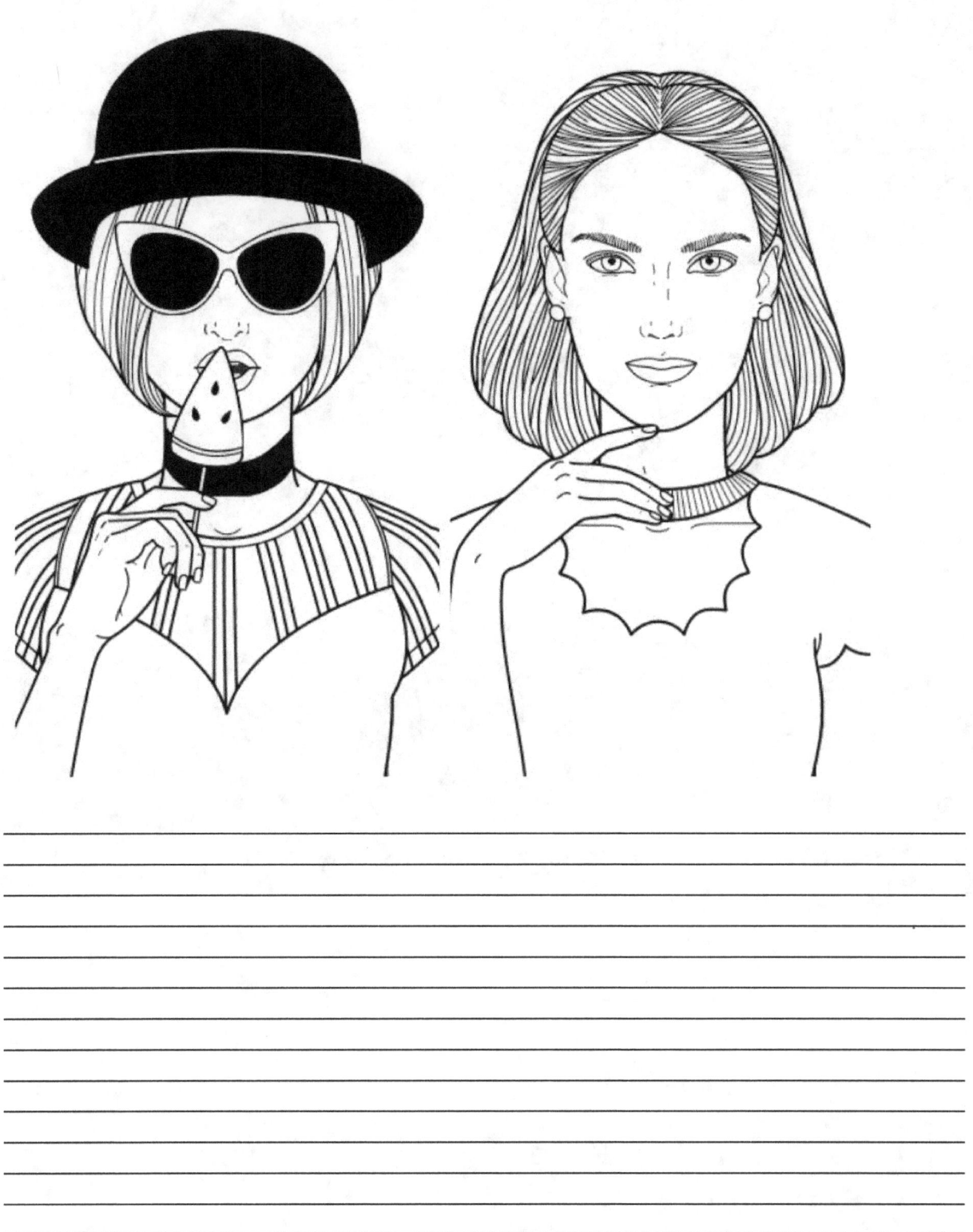

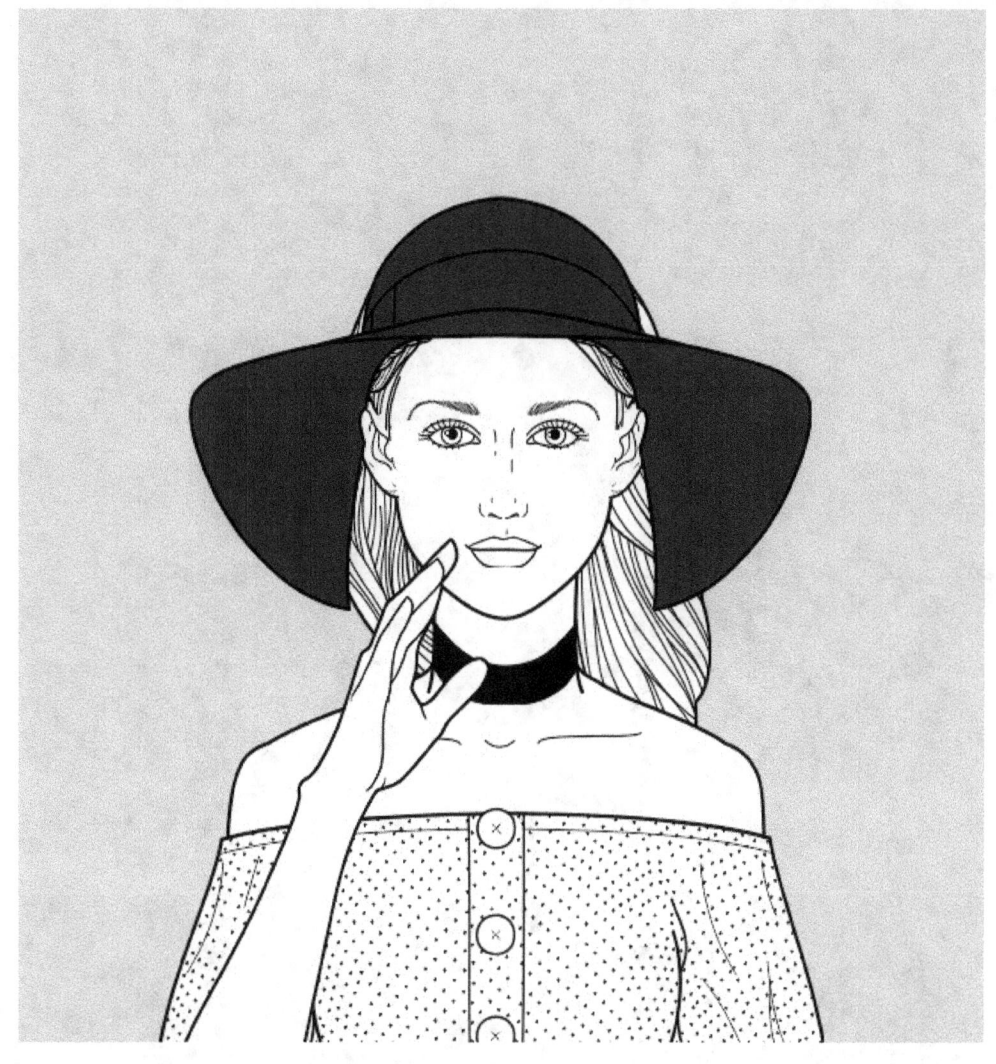

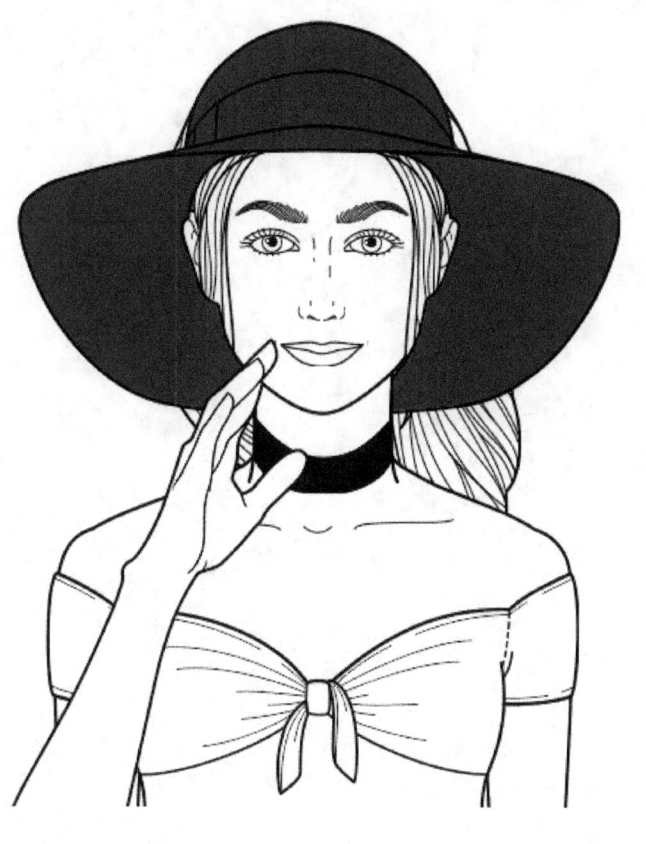

_____
_____
_____
_____
_____
_____
_____
_____

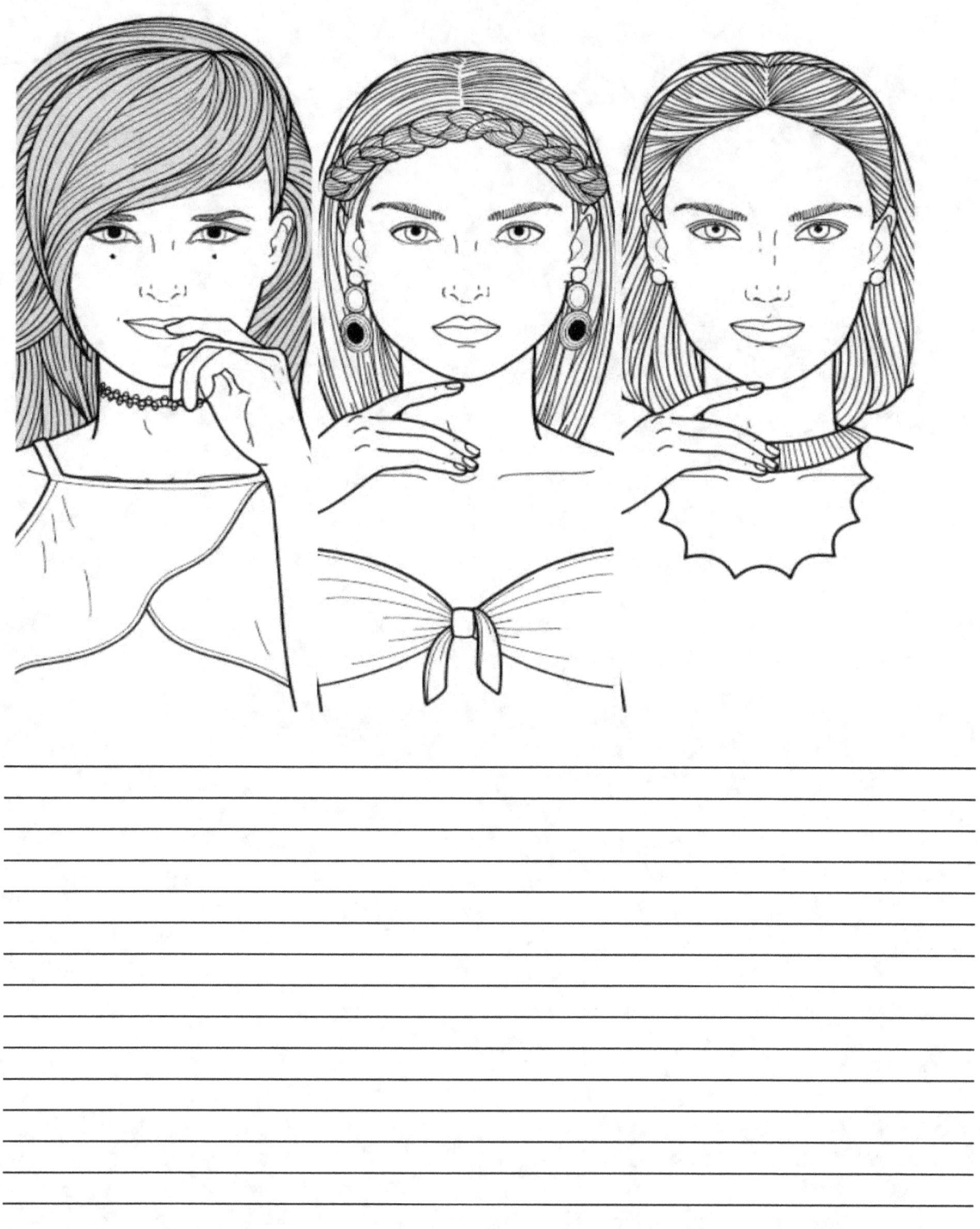

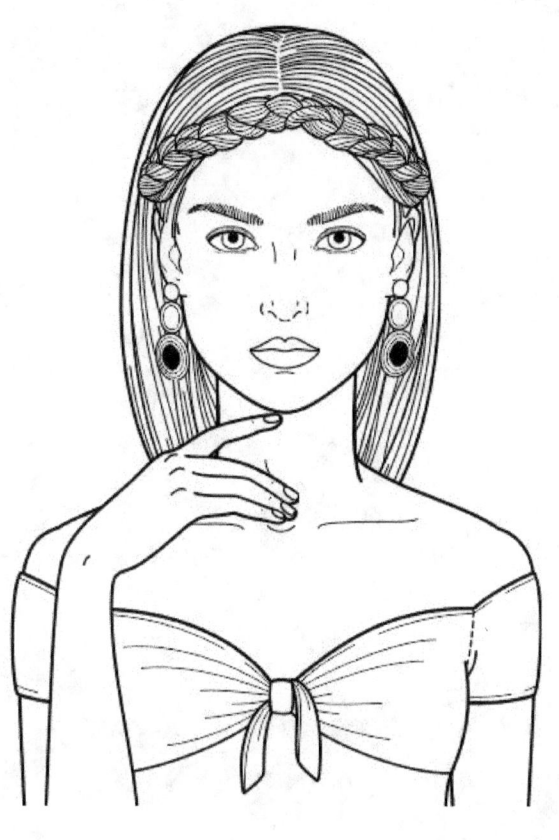

_____
_____
_____
_____
_____
_____
_____
_____

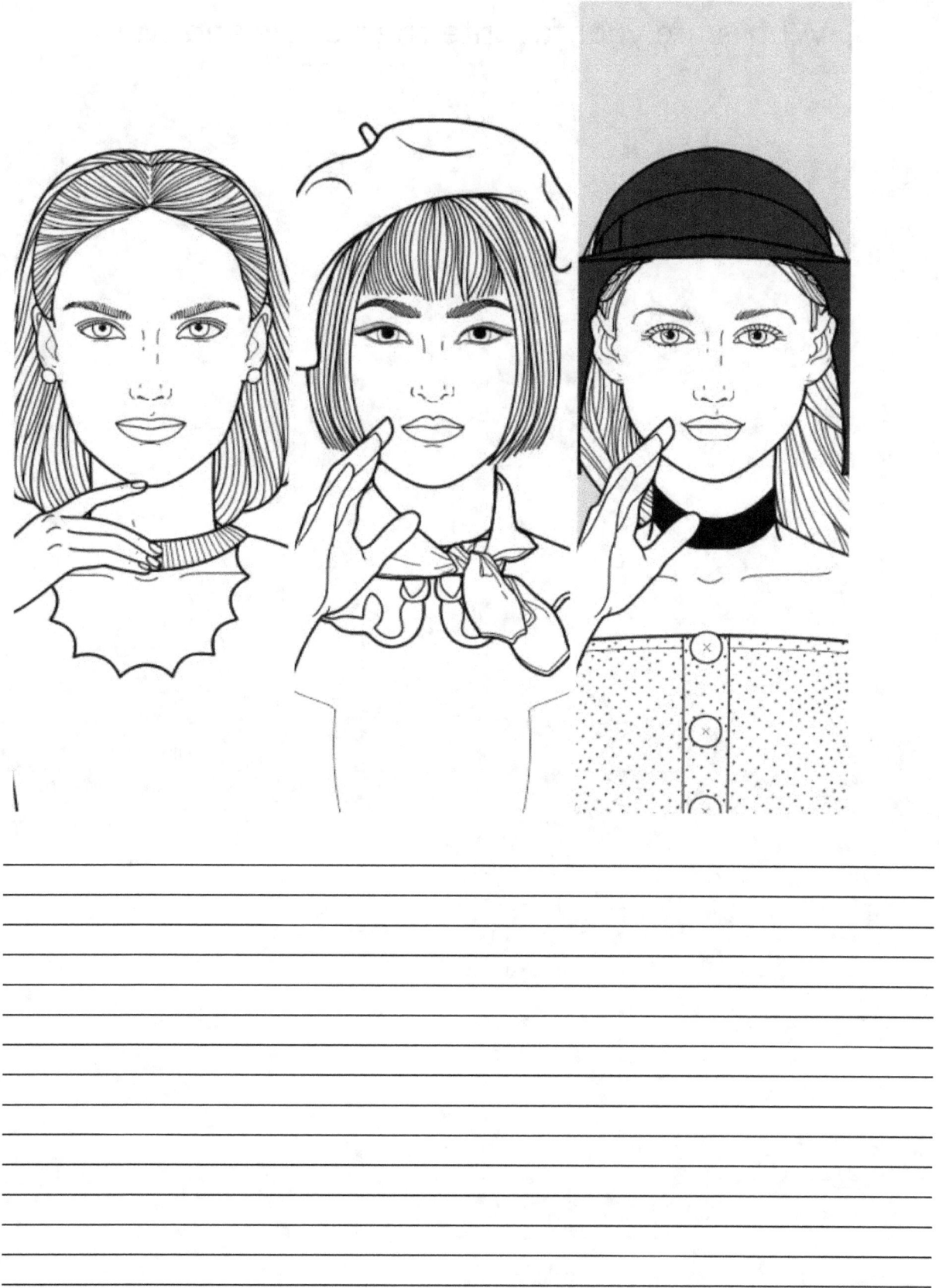

Who is/are your favorite character/s and why?

www.ingramcontent.com/pod-product-compliance
Lightning Source LLC
Chambersburg PA
CBHW081454220526
45466CB00008B/2642